# STORIES
# OF
# SUPERNATURAL
# HEALING

# BOOKS BY SID ROTH

*The Incomplete Church*

*There Must Be Something More*

*They Thought for Themselves*

## ALSO BY LINDA JOSEF, PH.D.

*Supernatural Healing—Stories of the Miraculous*

**AVAILABLE FROM DESTINY IMAGE PUBLISHERS**

# STORIES OF SUPERNATURAL HEALING

## Signs, Wonders, and Miracles

SID ROTH & LINDA JOSEF, PH.D.

DESTINY IMAGE® PUBLISHERS, INC.
P.O. Box 310, Shippensburg, PA 17257-0310
*"Speaking to the Purposes of God for This Generation and for the Generations to Come."*

This book and all other Destiny Image, Revival Press, MercyPlace, Fresh Bread, Destiny Image Fiction, and Treasure House books are available at Christian bookstores and distributors worldwide.

For a U.S. bookstore nearest you, call 1-800-722-6774.
For more information on foreign distributors, call 717-532-3040.
Reach us on the Internet: www.destinyimage.com.

Trade Paper: 978-0-7684-3598-6
Hardcover: 978-0-7684-3599-3
Large Print: 978-0-7684-3600-6
E-book: 978-0-7684-9052-7

For Worldwide Distribution, Printed in the U.S.A.
1 2 3 4 5 6 7 8 / 14 13 12 11 10

# Table of Contents

# Introduction

## *Sid Roth*

When I became a believer in the 1970s, I was blessed to meet Kathryn Kuhlman, one of the great healing evangelists of our time. There was a unique spiritual quality about Kathryn. The Holy Spirit was more real to her than the things around her. She radiated the peace of God.

Kathryn was at the forefront of a real move of God that revitalized faith for healing in the Church. Praying for the sick with the laying on of hands was normal. Speaking in tongues was normal for believers, and the worship of people singing together in tongues was truly breathtaking in its beauty. At altar calls many of those who said the prayer of salvation were immediately baptized in the Holy Spirit.

Although I had an opportunity to work more closely with Kathryn, I did not take it. That was a major mistake! As a new Jewish believer, I thought all Christians believed what was in the Bible and that healing miracles were normal. But as time went on, I learned that, just as in Jesus' day, the traditions of man undermined the promises of God. Most people do not see the full manifestation of God's promises for healing.

It is like the old days before electricity was in common use. People could see lightning strikes so they knew there was power there, but they had no idea how to use it. Today, everyone in the developed world has electricity and can flip a switch to turn on lights. I want people to have their spiritual lights on too!

## My Passion—Report God's Miracles

God's promises for miracles, healing, and deliverance shine just as brightly today as they did when Jesus walked the earth in bodily form. For the past 35-plus years, it has been my passion to report the miracles that the Lord is doing today. And you know what? In all these years, I have never run out of people to interview.

Today I have written multiple books that have been translated into many languages and I host a weekly worldwide television program and an international outreach all based on the same theme—God is real; Jesus is the Jewish Messiah; and He moves in power in the world today. Belief in Jesus the Messiah is the doorway to eternal life.

## Two Kinds of Healing

Everywhere Jesus went, He healed people. Crowds went wild to get close to Him, to touch that healing power. Healing of physical and emotional illnesses is one of the most convincing demonstrations of God's presence and His love. A person who is supernaturally healed of a real physical illness is never the same.

Having talked with thousands of people who have experienced supernatural healing, it has become clear to me that there are two different kinds of healing. The first kind is the sudden miracle—a healing given to someone as a free gift, sometimes when they least expect it.

The second kind of healing comes from learning how to exercise faith in God's Word. There is life and power in God's Word. But you need to get that truth down deep inside you. Just thinking it is true is not enough. This is why meditating on God's promises is so important. To meditate means to mumble out loud. When the Word comes to life inside you, there is an explosion of power in your spirit.

The following are examples of each kind of healing.

# A Sudden Miracle

Sudden miracles are dramatic healings that can even recreate physical organs and other body parts. The Holy Spirit gives these gifts of healing as He wills. God often has a special purpose for these people, such as a future ministry or witnessing to others of His love.

For example, I recently interviewed a woman who had undergone a gastric bypass operation with disastrous complications. The surgeon had used a staple gun without staples in it, and damaged her inner organs. She eventually had her entire stomach removed. She was living by means of a feeding tube, but she was in such misery that she pulled it out. She did not want to live that way.

She was literally dying when she went to a healing meeting led by Billy Burke. Billy himself had a supernatural healing from brain cancer as a 9-year-old child.

### SHE WAS OVERCOME BY GOD'S SPIRIT.

When he prayed for this lady, she was overcome by God's Spirit and pinned to the ground for several hours. After a few hours, she was released from the ground, completely healed.

When she finally stood up, she was so hungry that she went to eat at the nearest restaurant, which happened to be McDonald's. She ate a Quarter Pounder with a large order of French Fries and a Diet Coke and felt great. Without a new stomach, she would have died from that meal!

She later had a sonogram with the same technician who had previously documented her stomach being removed. In the darkened room, the technician did not know who was on the table and was joking about seeing the food in her stomach. She said, "Turn on the light and see who you are examining!" When the technician realized the woman previously had no stomach, she went screeching into the hallway!

## Healing Through Believing God's Word

The second kind of healing is based on the faith of the individual believer in the promises of God. When people are able to get the truth in God's Word down deep inside, they are healed either gradually or suddenly of their affliction.

Today, thousands of people are witnesses to the power of belief in God's Word to heal, and I have spoken directly with a great many of them. In many cases, their testimonies are recorded and available at no cost to you on our Website, www.SidRoth.org.

We have also written a book (*Supernatural Healing—Stories of the Miraculous,* Volume 1 of this series) in which we relate the experiences of some of those who found supernatural healing by having believed and spoken God's Word over their situation. Healing of strokes, cancer, drug addiction, and more has been experienced by thousands who trusted in God's promises.

One example we write about in *Supernatural Healing* is Dale Raatz. Dale's wife, Pearl, had a devastating stroke, and the doctors gave her little chance of surviving. If she did survive, the doctors said she would never regain consciousness due to the extensiveness of her brain damage.

Dale refused to stop speaking the promises of God over her, and continually spoke them out while seeking to hear God's plan for her recovery. To make a long story short, Pearl was completely healed and today works with him in their ministry. There is life in God's Word! God's werd is Already Bless, so now Let it bless you

## There Must Be Something More

The promises of healing are for all believers. Although many have believed and found healing, not everyone who has sought supernatural healing has been able to find it. Many have told me of their experiences seeking healing—they seemed to do everything, but healing was not manifested.

Do not be discouraged! Be persistent in your search for healing. God wants all of us to have the full benefits of salvation. Healing is as much a right for believers as forgiveness of sin and eternal life.

Note: We are not recommending you ignore any doctor's instructions or discontinue taking any prescribed medication. Ignoring a doctor's instructions or quitting medication all at once can be dangerous. We do not recommend this.

## What This Book Is About

I have been on a quest to understand what it is that blocks healing as well as other supernatural manifestations. God has led me to the work of several people who have made important contributions to understanding roadblocks to complete healing. This book has been written to share their insights with you.

These pages are full of supernatural feats of normal Christians who have been flooded with the power of a supernatural God. They are so full of the Spirit of God that they leak. And people are healed, delivered, and saved when they put their teachings into practice.

Ana Mendez Ferrell brings examples of the power of Communion to heal all sorts of illnesses. Dr. Paul Hegstrom explains the power of the spoken word to reprogram the mind for healing from abuse. Dr. Art Mathias reveals how hidden bitterness in the heart can be a roadblock to healing, and Katie Souza describes how the glory light of Jesus can be a source of healing. As you read these stories, your faith will grow.

## He Will Do for You

Remember, God is not a respecter of persons. That means that what He did for the people you are going to read about, He is ready, willing, and able to do for you. In fact, He wants you healed more than you want to be healed. Reading our first book, *Supernatural Healing,* and this book, gives you a broad picture of the different methods God could use for healing.

You cannot put God in a box. You cannot confine God to a formula. God has a unique way for you to receive your healing. His direction comes from intimacy with Him. It's time for you to ask to enter the secret place (Holy of Holies). How long will it take? It's up to your hunger. But the good news is Jesus is ready to return. He is accelerating everything.

My prayer for you while reading this book is that it will help you find your healing. I am completely convinced that we should all walk in the fullness of God's promises. Physical and emotional healing are as much part of the *Good News* as forgiveness of sin.

Chapter 1

# The Power in Communion
## *Ana Mendez Ferrell*

*He who eats My flesh and drinks My blood*
*abides in Me and I in him* (John 6:56).

A na Mendez Ferrell has seen more of the supernatural than most people alive today. In her ministry she has seen four people raised from the dead, countless mentally ill people set free, all kinds of diseases healed, and whole families saved. In addition, she has been supernaturally given the ability to speak four languages as well as prophetic gifts. Her story is remarkable, and her teaching is life-changing.

Most importantly, God has revealed to Ana how to take the Lord's Supper in a way that brings spiritual strength and bodily healing. Of Ana's revelation, it is interesting to note that Jesus spent the night before His crucifixion with His disciples at a Passover meal—what we now call the Lord's Supper, or Communion. He told His disciples that the bread was His body broken for their sins, and the wine was His blood, sealing the covenant of forgiveness. He told us that His body is real food and His blood is real drink. If our spirits don't take in their needed food and drink, is it any wonder we are weak?

The first church was Jewish, and they understood the power of the Passover feast. This understanding has been lost through the ages. I have often said that when the church began to depart from her Jewish roots, much of her power was lost.

As we move toward the goal of One New Man (Jew and Gentile together in Messiah Jesus), we are bringing the Gentile church back to her Jewish roots. This is leading to a mighty increase in miracles and bodily healing. Ana's teaching about the Lord's Supper is one of the most life-giving messages you can hear.

## Ana Saw Jesus

Ana was born in Mexico City. At the age of 18 she had little interest in religion and was not particularly seeking Jesus. However, He was seeking her, and she had a supernatural encounter with Jesus Himself: "I was in my bedroom at home, preparing for a school test. It was late in the afternoon when I looked out of the window and saw something very unusual. I saw a bright star shining in the midst of dark clouds. I approached the window to get a better look.

"Suddenly, from a star came a brilliant beam of light. In the middle of this beam, Jesus was standing in amazing glory. His grace and love were so powerful that the impact threw me to the floor. I was overwhelmed by the experience of His love. Then I heard Jesus say to me, '*You will be My servant. I will be your Lord, and you will know Me in its due time.*' I wrote these things down before I could forget them or become confused about what had happened. From that time on I was absolutely in love with Jesus."

## The Devil Tried to Destroy Her

Ana began an intense spiritual search to be reunited with Jesus, as she had seen Him in the vision. However, she could find no Christian to guide her. No one she knew could relate to her experience with Jesus. Although she attended Catholic services every day, she did not find what she was seeking. There were barely any non-Catholic churches in Mexico in those days, and she didn't know any spiritual leaders.

After a long period of searching, she came upon a man who professed to be an "enlightened one," who said he would guide her into spiritual truth. She says, "This man was really a witch doctor—a warlock. He had a powerful, hypnotic spirit and a fascinating intellectual ability.

"He was able to talk in a very compelling manner about all the mysteries of the universe and even about the Bible; he was very attractive to listen to. He had many Catholic icons around him and other trappings of religion, so I wrongly believed He was a Christian.

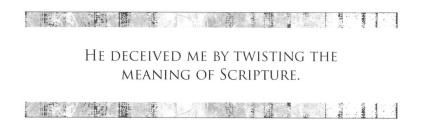

## HE DECEIVED ME BY TWISTING THE MEANING OF SCRIPTURE.

"I told him that I wanted to know Jesus. He said, 'Of course I can help you. I will be your spiritual guide.' He then opened the Bible and read John chapter 3. Twisting the meaning of Scripture, he told me I needed to be born again to enter into the Kingdom of God. He called the Kingdom of God the 'kingdom of magnificent magic.'

"He said, 'We must first give your life to the spirit of death—so you can die to this world system.' Then he led me through a dark, mysterious ritual in which I became demon possessed. I fell into the trap that had been set for me by the devil. The mental and spiritual horrors produced by the hosts of hell dragged me into mental illness and all kinds of sickness. All I knew after that was that there was no way out.

"The devil is a deceiver, and he will try to destroy you if you let him have a hook into your life. That's what he did to me, even though I did not want anything to do with him.

"He can get his hook into you through palm reading, Ouija boards, and other seemingly harmless things—even if you do not believe in these things. I urge all believers not to get mixed up with any kind of new age or occult practice, particularly those that have Christian trappings."

## Tormented by Demons

After this experience Ana was tormented by demonic spirits. A spirit of death drove her to several suicide attempts. After one of the most serious ones in which she cut her veins, she was taken to the hospital and was very near death. Ana recalls, "While I was in the emergency room, I heard the audible voice of God, as clearly as if someone were speaking to me saying, *'Your Father in Heaven will not forsake you.'* When I heard that, a tremendous supernatural peace came into me."

After she left the emergency room, Ana was sent to a mental hospital with a lifetime commitment. "If I had not been suicidal before I went there, that place was so terrible it would have made me so. At my lowest point, a pastor came to see me."

## A Vision of the Messiah

"This pastor spoke to me about Jesus being the Way, the Truth, and the Life. I could sense a light coming out of him. Something very real and truthful filled the atmosphere. As he prayed, the power of God came into me and clarity suddenly hit my mind.

"I said, 'I want to be saved.' He said that first I must repent. That one word produced an earthquake within me. The conviction of the Holy

Spirit invaded my heart, and I fell on my knees crying before God for a very long time.

"At that moment I had a clear vision of the Messiah. He was on the cross. His wounds were talking to me, saying, *'It is because of you. Because of you, I have paid this price.'*"

## Hit With Power

"The forgiveness that came out of Jesus hit me with power. The glory of God washed over me and I was instantly delivered. I experienced peace such as I had never before known, and all the demons left. I was healed and was instantly a new person, totally set free. At that point I understood that it is not knowing *about* Jesus that saves, but it is *following* Him and *obeying* Him. The devils know who Jesus is and they fear and tremble, but they could never follow Him."

Ana wanted to share this peace with the other patients. The pastor said, "They can have it. If you believe, the signs will follow! You will cast out demons and heal the sick." Ana and the pastor went throughout the mental hospital, door to door, and prayed for all the patients. Miracles hit many of the people, and they were delivered from demons and restored to their right minds.

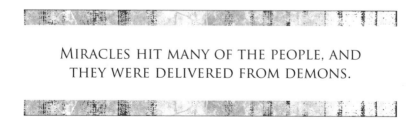

MIRACLES HIT MANY OF THE PEOPLE, AND
THEY WERE DELIVERED FROM DEMONS.

Ana was eventually released from the hospital. After she left, the chief psychiatrist called her, asking to know more about what had happened.

She was invited to return several times to the hospital to pray for some of the more seriously disturbed patients to be healed.

## Ana Receives Supernatural Gifts

Ana was just beginning her miraculous journey. Next she received supernatural gifts of languages—the ability to fluently speak English, French, Portuguese, and German, without ever having studied them.

Pastor Morris Cerullo was coming to Mexico City for an evangelistic meeting, and he needed interpreters who could speak both English and Spanish. Ana's sister heard the Lord say that she and Ana were to be interpreters at this conference. "When my sister told me about God's word to her, I said immediately that it was out of the question because I knew just a few words of English. The only language I had ever spoken was Spanish.

"My sister said, 'If God is saying you are one of the interpreters, is not the Holy Spirit able to supernaturally give you the language instantly on the platform?' This was not my sister talking; it was God! And I knew I had to agree to do it.

"When the evening came and the preacher I was to translate for was to speak, I stepped onto the platform just trusting for an awesome miracle. Then Heaven opened up and the English language came to me supernaturally, and I translated perfectly. Afterward, I had perfect command of English, and still do to this day. The Lord is able to do amazing things."

Not only was Ana given perfect command of English, she also received the same gift to fluently speak several other languages as well.

As Ana has matured in her faith, she has been led into a truly supernatural ministry that includes raising the dead and prayer against evil spirits that rule over nations and cities. She has learned to live her life in

Jesus and to keep strong in the Spirit through taking the Lord's Supper, Communion, every day.

## The Importance of Communion

Ana says, "The same Jesus who moves in me moves in you. But there is a thief who steals that power away from you, and that is wrong teaching about Communion. The greatest inheritance that Jesus left the Church is in Communion, and we have made it a ritual rather than a life-giving meal. We have lost that truth. The Holy Spirit is restoring that truth, and it is changing lives.

"Jesus says, *'Eat My flesh and drink My blood.'* We must understand this because it is Communion that lets us partake of all that Jesus did for us. We must learn that when we partake from it, the blood of Jesus is literally invading us at the spiritual level and filling us with Himself.

"The Messiah's followers understood the bread and wine of Communion were to be their spiritual food and drink. That is why the early Church observed it every day. In John 6, Jesus says, *'My flesh is real food, and My blood is real drink'* (John 6:55 NIV). It makes sense that we will grow weak and even sick without the proper nourishment for our spirits."

## Communion—Key to Divine Health

"The key to divine health—to never getting sick—is in Communion. In my spirit, I have drunk from the blood of Jesus. I know the price He paid to heal our sicknesses. Jesus came to bring the Kingdom of God, and the Kingdom of God provides perfect health.

"My husband and I travel all over the world, going to dangerous places and eating all kinds of food. We live in divine health. When I feel sick, I take Communion. The power of the blood of Jesus, of what He paid for us, is so effective that there is no disease that can stand against it."

## Communion Links Heaven and Earth

"Communion is a link that unites Heaven to earth, opening the door of the supernatural. Communion is the means by which the Lord imparts His nature and His power into our spirits.

"As we drink in His blood, the light of His life fills our veins. As we allow the blood of the Messiah to fill our spirits with light, we are creating the same connection with the supernatural that occurred when Yeshua (Jesus) was raised from the dead."

In her book about Communion, *Eat My Flesh and Drink My Blood,* Ana describes a glorious vision that changed her life when she was meditating on the Lord while taking Communion. In the vision, her spirit was carried to the Holy of Holies in Heaven where she saw the Ark of the Covenant. It was shining with energy, like a dense, churning fire with rays of light flashing out of it.

As she gazed on the Ark, she saw the Son of God enter this holy place, surrounded by a cloud of shining glory. Hovering in front of Him was a formless shape like a floating, red liquid. She knew it was His blood. "I watched as He put this blood on the Mercy Seat between the two cherubim of the Ark. When He did this, an explosion of power was produced that shook everything in Heaven and earth as fiercely as if an atomic bomb had gone off."

## A River of Life Flowed

"Power rushed forth from the blood on the Ark and some of it hit me, as if thousands of volts of electricity were going through me. My entire body turned red as His blood filled every atom of my being. Just when I thought I would die from the force of this power, I heard a voice saying, *'My Father has received My blood and now it has united with His Spirit. Receive the life in My blood!'*

"When I came back from this experience, I never again thought of the blood of the Messiah as a ritual or a symbol. I now understand that the blood is meant to invade and fill me completely, filling up first my spirit, then my soul, and at last my body.

"I noticed a profound personal change. A vital river of the water of life had started flowing from my inner being, and I felt a surge in health and strength. Now, when I take the Lord's Supper, I meditate afterward, basking in the marvelous light that emanates from His life. I have experienced great unity with the Lord and dramatic miracles as a result."

## Manifesting His Blood Overcomes the Devil

"I have learned the blood of the Messiah is life and light that is visible in the spiritual world. Darkness is the absence of light; it is the realm of the devil. Just as a fish needs water to live, the devil needs darkness to survive. When we drink the blood of the Messiah, His light runs through our veins and fills us with light so that we become a fearful adversary for the devil."

Ana believes that knowing this light fills us is key to overcoming the devil. "It is not enough to simply speak of the blood. What we must do is manifest the blood that fills our spirits. This is what overcomes the devil."

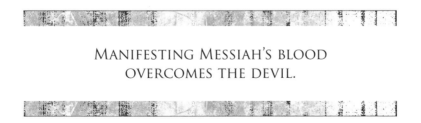

MANIFESTING MESSIAH'S BLOOD
OVERCOMES THE DEVIL.

To illustrate this power, she describes an occasion in which a monstrous demonic presence came into her room. "It was the devil himself. When I asked the Holy Spirit what to do, He told me to *manifest* the power of the blood. I felt the power of the Spirit of life surge out of my body like a force and literally hit the devil. He disappeared in seconds!

"Although the image of the devil was hideous, what the devil was seeing in me was much more scary. This power came from the blood of Communion. The life is in the blood, and when you take in the blood of Jesus into your spirit, you become so filled with His life that no demon can stand near you. Partaking of His blood and His flesh leads to a deeper knowledge of God as His life invades our being. It penetrates and fills our spirits, then transforms our souls and floods every cell of our bodies. The power of His resurrection is at work in us, transforming us at every level."

## Sacrificial Love Comes With the Blood

"There is also a sacrificial love that is beyond understanding as you drink of His blood. Every pore of your body starts to exude the power of forgiveness toward one another. This is why the Jerusalem church was in such unity that they put all their property in common. Love is the nature of the Father who gave His Son. As we drink of that blood, we start to be ourselves in the habit of sacrificial love.

"Those who have united with Messiah have become One Spirit with Him. While the early church was doing this, the fear of the Lord was present with all of them, and they had the favor of the people. They were gaining righteousness, and reflecting it into the world around them. Communion is transformative."

## We Become One With Him

"Our purpose is to know God, and to love the Messiah with all of our hearts. We must become one with Him. It is not about the intellect, thinking, or mentally knowing Him. It is about becoming one with Him. We need to raise up a generation of people who become one with Jesus through the observance of Communion.

"We *are* the Body of Messiah, and there is not one glory for the head and another for the arms, legs, and so on. Everyone who believes should be able to do the same works of power in His name.

"Pray for the eyes of your understanding to be enlightened, so that you can see the riches of the glory. This will happen as you have Communion every day and become connected with your brothers and sisters in the church."

## Communion Brings Healing

"The greatest inheritance that Jesus left the Church is in Communion. It is the power released from the cross of Calvary that heals sickness. I have drunk from this Spirit and know that He paid the highest price for us. His wounds speak—His blood cries out to us. We can live in divine health because of the power of the blood of Jesus. The price He paid for us is so incredible—this is part of His gift to us. The power of His blood causes extraordinary miracles."

## Alzheimer's Disease Suddenly Healed

"Communion has the power to restore health, and we can take it daily for ourselves and for our family members, no matter what their problem is. Jesus' forgiveness covers everything. There are many, many examples of people receiving healing as they took communion.

"On one occasion, a group met to pray for a man so ill with Alzheimer's disease that he was confined to his bed. The group had listened to my teaching on Communion, and they were playing my worship CD, *The Power of His Blood.*

"When they took Communion together in his home, something very dramatic happened. The power of that Communion reached right upstairs where the man was resting and healed him of his disorder. He got up out of his bed, and came walking down the stairs, saying, 'I am a new person.' He was totally healed of Alzheimer's disease.

"It is Communion that brings the power of the blood of Jesus on the scene."

## We Must Be Filled With His Blood

Ana teaches that God wants to give this glory to all of us. He does not want to just give it to a few special ones. The key is to understand the tremendous importance of Communion.

"The blood is a real, spiritual substance, not just a symbol that we think about and talk about. When we take Communion, we must allow our spirits to literally drink in His blood. We must allow ourselves to be invaded by the blood of Jesus. This blood fills you and becomes one with your blood. It will then scorch any demon that comes against you.

"The power of the blood of Jesus is so incredibly intense. We cannot experience this power just by talking about it. We must drink it in. It is strong. Communion is not a ritual or a memorial. It is a deliberate act of drinking the blood in our spirits. As we drink the fruit of the vine, our spirits drink the blood of Jesus. That is our true nourishment, and we should not try to live without it."

## Communion Brings the Power of Heaven

"Many are weak in spirit because they do not take the elements as true drink and true bread. Our spirits need to take in the fruit of the vine and the fruit of the earth, the body and blood, every day in order to truly possess His life. Communion brings the power of Heaven down to earth. I do this every day to feed my spirit, and when I feel a sickness coming on, I do it as a medicine.

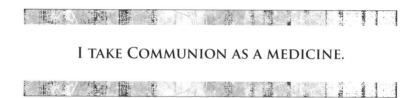

## I TAKE COMMUNION AS A MEDICINE.

"Doctors are a remedy when needed and as a last resource, but I have learned that there is a higher way, a truth that heals. Last year I discovered a growth in my body. But I chose to address it through Communion.

"When I take Communion as a medicine, I meditate on His body taking in His wounds all my infirmities. I see those wounds open up and I take them into myself. I make them mine with all the healing power they contain. I told Jesus, 'Not one drop of your blood, not one of your wounds will be in vain in my life.' I took Communion twice in this manner, and the growth disappeared. The power of the wounds of Jesus is so intense— nothing made by man could be more effective."

## Raised From the Dead

The first person Ana saw raised from the dead was her own daughter. She was 11 years of age and was jumping into a pool full of Styrofoam balls, such as they have in restaurants and play areas. As Ana's daughter was playing, the balls scattered and she fell on her neck and was dead instantly.

Ana picked up her daughter's lifeless body and started proclaiming the power of resurrection. The power of resurrection was so real to her from taking Communion, that when she proclaimed it, the power of life came back into her daughter and she was brought back from death.

Ana said, "Terminal diseases must bow before the power of His wounds, but it is not in pleading the power of His blood—it is in knowing that by eating His flesh and drinking His blood that you will have life in yourself. By drinking His blood and eating His flesh, you become filled with His life and His light. As you do this every day, His love fills you and drives out any affliction.

"The power that breaks the chains and sets the captives free is in the blood. As you participate in Communion daily, sins you have struggled with for years will just drop off. Communion is your vitamin, your medicine, your remedy. Take it and be healed."

(Note: We are not recommending you ignore any doctor's instructions or discontinue taking any prescribed medication. Ignoring a doctor's instructions or quitting medication all at once can be dangerous. We do not recommend this.)

## Closing Thoughts

In the last section of her book, *Eat My Flesh and Drink My Blood,* Ana addresses the bread of Communion. She reminds us of the powerful symbolism of bread throughout the Old and New Testament, and how Jesus said He is the Bread of Life, and the Bread that came down from Heaven (see John 6:33,35,48,51).

When we take the bread of Communion, we are eating the very Bread of Heaven and the Bread of Life. This Bread is broken for us as we contemplate His broken body. We are feeding our spirits as we do this. The study of John 6 is highly recommended for deeper insights about the body and blood of the Messiah.

When Ana prays, she says, "Lord, as we eat Your flesh, I call Your power to penetrate the bodies to heal every sickness—to let us eat from Your life and Your Spirit. Let our spirits become one with Your Spirit. I pray for the manifestation of a new generation who knows You and manifests Your power and Your Spirit. Thank you Jesus for what You paid on the cross of Cavalry, for Your magnificent sacrifice. I ask that everything You purchased for us will come to pass in our lives."

Ana's message to you: "The Lord has made a covenant that your family will be saved. We can call these family members into the Body of Messiah as we take in Communion. Every person in our family—those who were written from the foundation of the earth—we can call them by name into God's family. We can release the power of the Messiah Jesus over every person and command the powers of darkness oppressing them to release them. Our family members can be set free. We can command evil forces to leave them and the freedom of Heaven to enter their bodies and enter their souls."

* * *

Ana's book, *Eat My Flesh and Drink My Blood,* is one of the deepest studies of the Lord's Supper available. For more information about Ana Mendez Ferrell and her ministry, visit her Website at www.voiceofthelight.com.

Chapter 2

# Overcoming Domestic Violence
## *Dr. Paul Hegstrom*

*…when I became a man, I put away childish
things* (1 Corinthians 13:11).

M any people have seen the movie *Unforgivable,* starring John
Ritter. This movie portrays the life of Dr. Paul Hegstrom—his
descent into domestic violence and his God-inspired journey to overcoming this destructive behavior. Paul overcame domestic violence
and used what he learned to found a ministry for helping others get
free.

Paul had experienced childhood sexual abuse that left him feeling
ashamed and different from others. He began acting out destructive
behavior patterns that intensified over many years until ultimately, he
faced a prison term for domestic violence. With God's help, he avoided
prison and found a way to bring about lasting change.

Paul has learned that the emotional trauma some people experience in childhood can short circuit the brain, causing emotional development to freeze up. When this happens the person may become
trapped in self-destructive behavior, abuse, or addictions. Paul has
found biblical tools for healing childhood damage and restoring emotional heath.

# I Was an Abuser

When it comes to domestic abuse and rage reactions, Paul knows what he is talking about because he has lived it. He describes himself as having been "as foul a wife-abuser as anyone can imagine. From the first days of our marriage," Paul said, "I was an abuser. We were very young when we married—I was 19 and she was 16. Even dating I had shoved my wife around and mistreated her emotionally. I could not understand my sudden fits of anger, and never knew what was wrong with me—I felt flawed, dirty, and damaged.

"Thinking that stability would help me get hold of my emotions, I had insisted we marry even though she was still in high school. On the second day of marriage, I went off on her physically. I hated myself for doing it, and apologized profusely, but I did it again and again over the sixteen years of our first marriage.

"I prayed to God to help me, but God seemed indifferent, never answering my urgent prayers, listening to others, but not to me. My father was a minister, and I could see that God did answer prayers of others, but to me, He was totally silent."

# I Suffered Childhood Sexual Abuse

"God was silent to me because satan had gotten to me through sexual abuse outside the family. I had been raped by a neighborhood boy when I was 8½ years old. I had tried indirectly to tell my mother of this terrible experience, but she did not understand my veiled communication. She thought I was trying to talk about sex and washed my mouth out with soap.

"I was left to deal with it alone. I had a terrible sense of shame and felt dirty and damaged. I lost my sense of safety, my trust in my parents, and every shred of self-worth I had.

"The shame carried on from this childhood experience led me to handle another situation inappropriately. I was 13 and was in a photographic darkroom at a new school when a teacher's assistant began to molest me. I froze and did not cry out. I was emotionally paralyzed and could not move. This continued for the entire school year. Frightened and ashamed, I said nothing about it to anyone."

## Hiding Behind a Nice-Guy Image

"The effect of this abuse on my self-image was devastating. Inwardly, I felt dirty and different from the other kids. I was seething with rage. However, I covered it up with an outward personality that was likable and polite.

"I was nice when I had to be, but I could not keep the rage from spilling out. I got into fights at school and frequently used foul language. I became known for my hostile and aggressive attitude.

"I had a dual personality from my teen years on. My dad was a pastor, and at home I was the model child. I acted so polite to my parents that when people reported my bad behavior to them, they could not believe it. That's how good my deception was."

## Desperate to Escape From Myself

"I was desperate to escape from my unmanageable emotions. I pressured my girlfriend, Judy, to marry me at a young age, hoping that marriage and stability would help me take hold. But by the second day of our marriage, I could not control my anger, and threw her against a wall. Any time Judy did not meet my expectations, I was merciless in criticizing her, and often allowed it to escalate to physical violence.

"I not only hit her physically, I abused her emotionally, spiritually, mentally—in just about every way there is. I trained her to be a victim, telling her that she was lucky to have any man because she was so ugly and stupid—all the things that she was not. As a young woman, she was brilliant—smarter than me—so I had to put her under. I have found that this is a very typical pattern in domestic violence. Also part of the pattern is the deep remorse the day after. I can't count how many times I apologized and promised never to do it again.

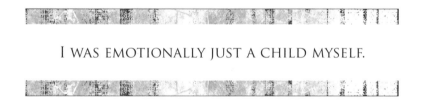

I WAS EMOTIONALLY JUST A CHILD MYSELF.

"By the time our two children came along, I was totally overwhelmed with the responsibilities of parenting and family life. I was emotionally just a child myself. I have since learned that the more you hate yourself, the higher your expectations are for your partner, and the more enraged you become when they don't measure up.

"I hated who I was in this relationship. I totally blamed my wife and my circumstances for my anger. I left her several times and eventually divorced her."

## Others Paid the Price for My Pain

"There is no question that my family paid the price for my childhood hurts, particularly my wife. She was loyal and tried to hide what I was doing from her family, but the physical battering, humiliation, and insults devastated her sense of self-worth.

"Due to my own insecurity, I needed to control everything she did, so she had no friends and no freedom to make decisions that I did not jump in and criticize. She became frightened to speak and ashamed of what I made her endure. She was isolated and fearful, and that was the way that I, in my sickness, wanted it. I did not want her to have any options other than me."

## I Failed at Every Job

"At work, I would not take responsibility for my actions—everything was someone else's fault. Drinking was also a problem. Sooner or later, I would quit the job and move on, hoping that a fresh start would make a difference. We moved so often that my wife finally got to where she would not even unpack the boxes.

"I even thought I could be a pastor. I hoped that going into the ministry would help me mature, and that more responsibility would help me settle down and be a good family man, but it had just the opposite effect. I was more abusive than ever, and what was worse, my congregation knew it."

## Escaping Into More Violence

"I was disgusted with myself, but I blamed my wife, Judy. I decided to leave her and divorced her without her knowledge. I was looking for something else with someone else.

"I had a series of failed relationships. However, I eventually found a woman who would put up with me and we moved in together.

"This was a big mistake. I wound up beating her so severely that she nearly died. As a result, I was facing 15-22 years in prison on charges of attempted murder. At the time, I was living in Minnesota, a state that was particularly tough on abusers. I still remember my lawyer saying to me, 'Man, you are the stupidest criminal I have ever represented. You have beaten up a woman in the state that has arguably the stiffest possible penalties for domestic violence.'"

## I Finally Accepted Responsibility

"I was terrified of going to prison, and promised myself that I would die before I would go through that. I was at the end of my rope. I threw myself on my face and cried out to God. I blamed everyone but myself, but I begged God to help me.

"Late on a February night in the early 1980s, I threw myself completely on His mercy. I said, 'God, if you can do something with me, I'm yours. I give you my finances, my sexuality, and everything I am.'

"There is more to the story, but I was saved from prison. It had to have been a supernatural deliverance, because I was set to go down for what I had done. I was offered a deal that allowed me to avoid prison in agreement for entering a treatment program.

"I tried that program for a year and spent almost $20,000 on counseling. I got medication and some skills for managing my emotions. I did not get the help I needed, but I did finally take responsibility for my actions. The problem was mine and mine alone.

"I had been blaming others and rationalizing my own reactions. I had not learned the crucial principle, *You are not responsible for your wounds, but you are responsible for your behavior.* I have now learned that there will be no change without first accepting responsibility."

## God Gave Me a Teachable Spirit!

"I continued to pray, to argue with God really, wanting to be bailed out without really changing. Eventually my will broke, and I received a message from the Holy Spirit. He said, 'You are not teachable. You are in rebellion, but if you will become teachable, the Father will give you a program that will restore your family, and you can take it to the world.'

"I surrendered completely to Jesus and to the way He wanted me to live my life. I began to diligently study the Bible. I responded to the simplicity of the Living Bible, and God drew me deeper into His Word and His promises and my life irrevocably changed. By studying the Scriptures and applying them to my life, I found healing and a new way of life.

"After seven years of separation and divorce, Judy and I began to rebuild our relationship. We developed a friendship first, and gradually Judy came to trust me again. With time and patience, God gave us a new love for each other and we remarried. We have now been remarried for 18 years.

"I have rebuilt relationships with my children. Our family is restored, and there is no abuse. It is completely gone. So much so, that when I tried to reenact some abusive scenes for the movie, *Unforgivable*, I was unable to even pretend to be an abuser!"

## God Kept His Promise

God was faithful to the promise that Paul would be given a program that he could take to the world. Although he had no background in mental health, God revealed things to him that have proven to radically change the lives of even hardened abusers. These concepts have formed the basis for Life Skills International, a ministry that Paul and his wife, Judy, offer for abusers and their partners.

Paul describes how the program works: "The program helps people to tie their symptoms together. Current struggles, divorce, anger, rage, acting out, no stability, changing jobs—all these symptoms have a source in inner wounding. Until that source is uncovered and healed, the person will remain stuck in an emotional dead zone. Usually a person can't uncover this source without help. We need direction and someone to tell us what is going on.

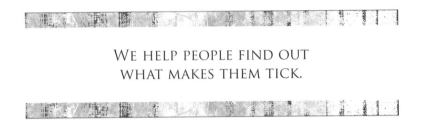

## WE HELP PEOPLE FIND OUT WHAT MAKES THEM TICK.

"In the Life Skills program, we help people find out what makes them tick. We cannot help the fact that we were hurt or damaged in some way. However, we are responsible for how we live out the rest of our lives. We are responsible for our current behavior, no matter how much we want to blame someone else.

"In this program, we uncover the original hurt. We give people directives and teach them, and with God's grace, help them take hold of their lives. We lead them into paths of repentance and forgiveness and inner healing. I am living proof that we can learn to overcome our past. No matter what our age or circumstances, we can change if we have the right tools."

## How to Overcome Explosive Anger

"One area where we see good success is in overcoming rage and violence. To overcome rage, we must use our conscious mind to interrupt the anger process. We do this by learning to recognize the warning signs or steps leading up to an explosive reaction. The instant we see one of the warning signs, we can interrupt the process by taking a time out, or walking away before it gets worse. This is how we stay in control.

"The earliest warnings of an impending explosion include the usual signs of stress such as tunnel vision, nausea, tight chest, and dry mouth. Next comes a sense of disorientation or possibly a feeling of detachment. This is often followed by accusing thoughts and picking a target. Anger, verbal insults, and intimidation come next, and quickly lead to throwing things and physical and emotional numbness.

"As the reaction escalates, the person starts to fantasize about violence and visualizes the attack. By this point, events are controlling the abuser, as if he or she is trapped on a runaway train. Threatening and screaming give way to loss of control and physical violence. At the end, there is little awareness of what he or she is doing and certainly no concern for the consequences.

"The key thing that we need to learn is to use our conscious mind to *stop* the process that our emotions have started up. Once we learn the warning signs or steps leading up to the explosion, we know we are in a process, and we can gain the ability to manage it. With practice, the conscious mind gets better at overcoming the emotions."

## Anger Masks Inner Pain

Paul teaches people that emotions cannot be trusted, even though they may "feel" very real. He explains, "Anger and rage are really masks for inner fear and emotional pain. We need to recognize that anger is not the true emotion but a cover-up or substitute. As the apostle Paul writes so often, we owe nothing to the flesh. We are not obligated to our emotions. They are not truth; they are just emotions.

"By understanding that the anger is a cover-up for some other issue, the person gains the confidence to interrupt it at any point in the process. Taking a deep breath, counting to 100, or just walking away are all ways of interrupting the process, allowing things to cool down. When we cool down, we can reconsider how best to approach the situation."

# Trauma Causes Arrested Development

Paul's approach is based on getting beneath the anger to heal the underlying hurt or pain. He explains, "There is a reason for destructive patterns. When trauma or emotional hurts occur in childhood, the emotional part of the personality stops maturing. The apostle Paul writes, *'When I was a child, I spoke as a child, I understood as a child, I thought as a child; but when I became a man, I put away childish things'* (1 Cor. 13:11). People who have been traumatized never grow up. They continue to think like children and to react like children.

"It has a lot to do with how a child's brain reacts to trauma. Before the ages of 9 to 11, important mechanisms regulating brain chemicals such as serotonin, dopamine, and norepinephrine are immature. Trauma causes important developmental processes to freeze in place, creating what psychologists call 'arrested development.'

"Arrested development means that the wounded child has learned to live in a state of tension, always waiting for the next event. The child does not move on developmentally because he is stuck, waiting for the next trauma. So even though the outward person continues to grow and mature, the inner person remains stuck in that immature childhood state.

"The person continues to mature outwardly, but she inwardly is holding on to childhood fears and rejection, basically remaining a child in an adult body. This accentuates the person's feeling that she is crazy or defective in some manner.

"The most typical causes of childhood trauma are abandonment, rejection, incest, molestation, and physical and emotional abuse. However, it does not take a big trauma to create this arrested development. To a vulnerable or sensitive child, even a normal or mild event can do damage if it has powerful meaning to the child."

# Developing a Pseudo Personality

"People with arrested development usually know that they are different from others. I think we instinctively know that something is not right in our functioning, so we develop an acceptable front to show to others. We develop a pseudo personality. In my case, people outside my home thought I was a great guy. I seemed really likable to the public.

"The likable pseudo personality is a façade, however. We cannot really love, cannot manage anger, and cannot parent effectively, because inwardly we are still children, frozen emotionally, waiting in fear for the next trauma. We tend to see other people as objects that either meet or don't meet our needs. And when we are disappointed, we react with anger, hurt, or rejection."

# Childhood Wounds Drive Destructive Behavior

"Childhood wounds are what really drive destructive behavior patterns. For example, my fear of being out of control led to my overbearing and dominating behavior toward my family. It was an unconscious, unthinking reaction that was meant to protect me from my feelings of helplessness."

The most common destructive behavior patterns involve the person feeling victimized, helpless, and angry. However, some people have destructive behavior patterns that play out the rescuer role in which the person looks for someone who is hurting worse than he is so he can rescue them. The person basically avoids getting hurt by focusing on taking care of someone else. The other person's needs are what he thinks about. This is the essential dynamic in codependence.

People with arrested development may not even know what they need or why they are upset, but that does not stop them from having high expectations of the other party. They may communicate their frustration with tantrums, explosive anger, or other emotional displays that seem out of place.

Paul describes how this affects relationships: "In a healthy relationship, we accept what our partner can give along with what she cannot give. In a dysfunctional relationship, we constantly challenge the other party to prove herself. Nothing ever gets resolved. Anger is not handled with maturity and love.

"Addictive relationships are common. An addictive relationship is one based on need, not on choice. People move from relationship to relationship hoping to get their emotional needs met, and always feeling disappointed. The idea that someone else can make things better for us when we are broken inside is unrealistic."

## How Wounded People See Things

"The viewpoints that people take of situations are what drive their emotional reactions, and each person has his own unique way of looking at events. For example, if two people were to sit across the table from each other, they could both be seeing the same coffee cup, but they would be seeing it from different perspectives.

"One person would see the handle on the left and the other would see it on the right. Neither of these perspectives would be inherently correct; they would be understandably different, but each person could think that he or she had the right perspective and that the other person's view was skewed.

"Our view of significant life events is similarly biased. When we are healthy, we recognize that there are different points of view in a situation. Wounding and emotional immaturity cause us to think *our* view is the *only* correct one."

# Inner Wounding Affects Perceptions

"Our perceptions are affected by our fears, insecurities, our lack of maturity, and our lack of self-value. For example, when a child is wounded through sexual abuse, her sense of self-value is established from her perspective. She is likely to believe that her value lies in being a sexual object and that she otherwise has no worth.

"When a child has been abandoned, the child may conclude that anyone he loves will leave him, therefore he dares not love. A child who has suffered criticism and rejection will interpret others' behavior as a continuation of that earlier rejection. As an adult, he will take comments and actions personally and will look for hidden agendas."

# Respecting Different Points of View

"Coming back to the coffee cup example, when we have a healthy mindset, we can acknowledge that whether the cup handle is on the right or on the left depends on how the person sees it.

"If we have a wounded or damaged mindset, our truth will be only how *we* see it. Our perception becomes our reality. When someone disagrees with our perspective, we tend to take it personally as if we are being insulted. We will fight to justify our perspectives no matter how warped they are.

"By the time we are adults our perceptions have become interwoven with our self-image, and we no longer can separate our perspective from our sense of self. We are our perspective and our perspective is the truth."

# God's Word Reprograms the Mind

The way we learn our perspective on life is part of what the Bible calls the natural person or the carnally minded person. Our brains are literally programmed with this learned perspective based on childhood hurts. Paul has found that lasting change requires not just controlling our behavior but reprogramming the way we think.

"The Life Skills Program uses the Word of God to bring about mental health. God never meant for us to fail. He meant for us to be healed and to mature into sanctified adults. The Creator has put a system like a computer inside us, in our brains. There is a hard drive that stores our memories and a software program that accesses those memories, tells us what they mean and how to react to the situations in which we find ourselves.

## THE GOD WHO CREATED OUR BRAIN KNOWS EXACTLY HOW TO HELP US FORM A SPIRITUAL MIND.

"The God who created our brain knows exactly how to help us form a spiritual mind. The Word of God is the ideal software for this reprogramming. It was written by our Creator to help us mature and make wise decisions as we grow in God.

"All we have to do is support the operation of that healthy software program by getting the Word of God down inside us, and importantly, by doing everything God's way. No matter what the problem is—pornography, sex, abuse, addictions, depression—it will eventually yield to God's Word if we allow God's Word to speak to our hearts."

## Truth Sets Us Free

"The Book of Hebrews says that the Word of God is a living thing, that it is powerful and able to divide soul from spirit. You can take the Word of God like a medicine and it will bring you health.

"The brain responds to truth. God put in our brain a truth checker, and the truth will set you free. When I was in counseling, I knew certain things were wrong. When God started dealing with me, I knew what was true. People know instantly when something is true—they see it. We cannot help changing once we see the truth."

## Meditate—to Mumble Out Loud

"God's written Word is the key to change. As we draw it into ourselves, it changes us by literally reprogramming our brain. To take full advantage of this life-giving quality in the Word of God, *it is important to not just read the Bible but to say the Bible words out loud.* The Hebrew word for meditate can be translated as to mumble out loud. We can meditate on God's Word by speaking it over and over to ourselves.

"There is power in the spoken word. The Creator *spoke* the world into existence, and He designed our minds, the ultimate computer, to respond to the spoken word as well. It is important to say words of the Bible out loud because when you are saying them, you are also hearing them, and this is powerful."

## Speaking Commits Us to Action

"There is a difference between thinking about a thing and speaking it out loud. When we think about doing something internally, it is an option, one of many possible things we might do. No actions are connected to it. However, when we speak it, we move the thought into a decision. When we speak a thing repeatedly, our brain comes into submission to it, and it will change. This is how we rewire the brain.

"Most of the negative thought patterns we have are what the Bible calls 'strongholds.' They are little fortresses in our brains that resist the truth of God. We have been babies long enough, falling for everything and standing for nothing. *It takes a real commitment to reading and speaking the Words of God to start the maturing process.* When reading the Bible, do not just read it internally. Read it out loud. As you read it, you are speaking with authority to bring down enemy strongholds.

"Your body also will come into submission to the words you speak. For example, I had open-heart surgery with complications that left me literally brain damaged. The doctor said I had lost about 40 percent of my capacity. I could see what I wanted to say in my mind but could not make it come out. I have completely regained my capacities, something that should be an encouragement to stroke victims.

# Bringing Down Strongholds

> *For though we walk in the flesh, we do not war according to the flesh. For the weapons of our warfare are not carnal but mighty in God for **pulling down strongholds,** casting down arguments and every high thing that exalts itself against the knowledge of God, bringing every thought into captivity to the obedience of* [Messiah] (2 Corinthians 10:3-5).

"By challenging our brain and speaking out the Word of God, we actually rewire the brain. As we read Scripture out loud, what is coming out of our mouth is taking authority over our body, bringing down the strongholds.

"Past programming will tempt us to choose an old pattern, but we have the ability to choose God's way. The Holy Spirit will show us what we need to change. Our minds will bring out all the options and try to work them out; but once we make a decision, we need to speak it out loud, saying, 'This is what I choose to do.'

"When we outline our options verbally, the steps we must take to put our decision into action become clearer. Billy Graham always tells people who accept Jesus to call a friend or family member, to find someone and tell them of their decision.

"At times of temptation, I say to myself, 'Paul Hegstrom, this is not an option for your life.' I am making a choice, speaking my commitment. I am bringing down strongholds with the word of my confession.

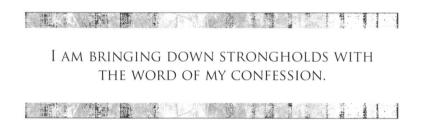

I AM BRINGING DOWN STRONGHOLDS WITH
THE WORD OF MY CONFESSION.

"In the Book of Revelation, there is a Scripture that says we overcome by the blood of the Lamb and the word of our testimony (see Rev. 12:11). Science is catching up with what is in the Bible. Our program has been very successful in creating lasting change with abusers. We have a major university ready to do brain scans on men with domestic violence problems at intake and after the Life Skills program to prove that God's Word actually changes the brain."

## Broken Children, Grown-up Pain

During his lifetime, Paul estimates that he has spent over $30,000 on mental health treatment that did not really help him. He reports that 97 percent of the abusers who come through his program achieve lasting change.

In his book *Broken Children, Grown-up Pain,* Paul describes some of the important mental health concepts that he has found to be effective. Paul says, "God does not intend for us to stay broken. He has designed a healing process that we can call sanctification, or we can call it emotional maturity.

"As we grow up, we can see people who are hurting more than we are, and we have something we can do to help them. We can extend a hand, grab them, and help them along. Then they are able to help others, and by this the Body of Messiah matures. Just remember that the Bible is your truth book, and you are going to know the truth, and the truth is going to set you free."

# What You Can Do

1. **Believe that there is healing for you in God**. God wrote a software program and designed your wiring to bring you back to health, balance, wholeness, and salvation. The Bible reveals His plan for your life.

2. **Trust in God**. Spend time in His Word, and open your heart to God. Read the Bible out loud so that your mind comes into submission to it, and tell Him you are sorry for every sin as it comes to mind.

3. **Make a decision to change**. We demolish arguments and every stronghold that sets itself up against the knowledge of God, and we take captive every thought to make it obedient to God (see 2 Cor. 10:5). You can choose to change your thinking and your behavior. Every time you resist an old habit pattern, you are helping to reprogram your brain with God's software.

4. **Speak your decisions**. There is power in the spoken word. Our Creator spoke the world into existence. He designed our minds to respond to the spoken word as well. We must learn the importance of speaking our decisions and commitments out loud. As long as we just *think* about a plan, it remains an option but not

a decision. When we outline our options verbally, the steps we must take to put our decision into action become clear. At times of temptation, I say aloud, 'Paul Hegstrom, this is not an option for your life.' I'm making a choice. I'm bringing down the strongholds. I'm bringing captive my imagination.

5. **Ask the Holy Spirit to lead you**. He will guide you in talking with a trusted friend to uncover the source of your pain.

\* \* \*

For more information about Dr. Paul Hegstrom and his ministry, visit his Website at www.lifeskillsintl.org. His book is titled, *Broken Children, Grown-Up Pain: Understanding the Effects of Your Wounded Past.*

Chapter 3

# Our Angelic Allies
*Pastor Ron Phillips*

*He shall give His angels charge over you, to keep*
*you in all your ways* (Psalm 91:11).

Although the New Testament contains more than 175 specific references to angels, most people know very little about these extraordinary beings. Ron Phillips has found that angels are here to help believers advance God's Kingdom, and that they play an important role in healing and protecting us from harm.

Ron pastors the 3,000-member church Abba's House in Chattanooga, Tennessee. He is a Bible scholar with solid, Fundamentalist training whose life and ministry were radically altered when God exposed him to the realm of the supernatural. He has been given unusual insight into this realm through scriptural study and direct experience.

Ron has an important message for you: "In these challenging times, it is clear that man is coming to the end of himself. We must learn to move in the full supernatural of God, and part of that is learning how to partner with angels. There is an unemployment crisis, but it is not with humans here on earth. It is among all the angels waiting around for believers to call on them for help!"

# Ron Meets His First Angel

Ron's first supernatural experience occurred more than 30 years ago when an angel saved his life and started him on a journey toward accepting the supernatural as an important part of the believer's experience.

He describes how it happened: "I was a young pastor, just 29 years old. I had driven in my car to preach a sermon on the top of a snowy North Alabama mountain. My wife had warned me not to go, due to the weather, but at the time, I was too young to realize that God sometimes speaks to you through your wife.

"The service went well, and when I had finished preaching, I started back down the mountain. It had gotten colder and the snow had picked up, but I thought I could make it. I had not traveled very far down the narrow and winding road when my car started skidding and did two 360s on the ice. When my car finally came to a stop, I was at the edge of a steep embankment, and could see 800 to 900 feet down. There was no way for the car to move without risk of going over the edge.

"I knew I was in trouble, and I instinctively cried out 'Lord, help me!' Then I heard His voice speaking to my spirit, saying, *'Your angel is sitting beside you. Command your angel to help you.'* I thought I could see a glowing form in the front seat beside me. Without thinking, I said 'OK… angel, will you please go outside and help me not skid and to get safely home!'

"I did this because I was so upset. Calling out to angels went against all my theology as a Southern Baptist. I had never really thought about the Scripture in Hebrews 1:14 that says, *'Are they not all ministering spirits sent forth to minister for those who will inherit salvation?'* I was a strict Cessationist and believed that all the supernatural things were passed away, that they were for the Bible times only. God was beginning to shake my tradition."

# A Glowing Presence

"As soon as I called out to the angel, the glowing light I had seen moved to the right front fender of my car. Somehow I knew it was safe to proceed, so I shifted the gear into drive, the tires gripped the road, and I made it down the mountain. As we rode down the mountain road, the light moved from outside to what looked like a glowing figure sitting in the car with me.

"When I finally rolled to a stop at the intersection of Interstate 59, I saw that a State Trooper had set up a barricade so nobody could go up the icy road. The Trooper said, 'How did you get down off the mountain?' And all I could think of to say was, 'Well, God helped me.'

"Then he looked in the car at me and over to the passenger side, and he said, 'You all be safe.' The way he talked, I could tell that he saw someone else in the car with me, which was a confirmation that I was not going crazy, but I was stunned. I drove the rest of the way home and did not know what to think."

Ron believed that one of God's angels came out of the eternal dimension into earthly time to rescue a young, frightened preacher. This was the beginning of 12 years of God's efforts to change the beliefs of a Southern Baptist pastor who believed that all the supernatural gifts had ceased.

# Angels—Our Invisible Allies

Ron has since learned that angels are a key connection between earth and the supernatural dimension. In his book *Our Invisible Allies,* Ron writes:

Beyond our normal range of understanding is another dimension more real and lasting than anything we can imagine. The existence of another realm called 'the heavenlies' where marvelous creatures both magnificent and malevolent operate is not science fiction. In this realm exist these living beings called angels, along with their dark cousins, demons. Created by God, these timeless beings have a history of their own. Remarkably, they have the ability to come and go between the eternal dimension and our world.[1]

"Angels are older than time. They saw what rebellion did to one-third of their host and they don't want it to happen to us. They know that even though Jesus won the war on the cross, there is a tremendous battle raging for the souls of humankind. They are our allies, and they want us to win. They take joy when we make the right decisions.

"The Bible says you will hear a voice behind you saying this is the way, walk ye in it. David says, 'Surely goodness and mercy will follow me, all the days of my life.' The angels are before us to prepare the way and are our rear guard."

## Angels All Around Us

Angels are all around us and serve many different purposes in God's Kingdom. They serve as messengers, as they did to Zacharias and Mary when they announced the birth of Jesus. Angels take physical action, as they did when they rolled the stone away from Jesus' tomb. They provide help in time of need, as they did when they released Peter from prison and appeared to Paul on the storm-tossed ship. Angels have a prominent role in the Book of Revelation, and also work to strengthen us as they strengthened Elijah and Jesus.

Angels came and ministered to Elijah when he was in the wilderness, and to Jesus after He was tempted by the devil. Ron has found that God often sends angels to minister to those who have been attacked.

"The Bible says that Jesus healed all who were oppressed by the devil. Diseases do not come forth from God but represent attacks on the children of God. In our church we have seen healing of cancer, deafness, diabetes, and many other diseases; and I believe that angels play a part in this.

GOD OFTEN SENDS ANGELS TO MINISTER TO
THOSE WHO HAVE BEEN ATTACKED.

"People often come down with things like stomach disorders and cancers because they are physically worn out. Sometimes our bodies are not strong enough to fight off whatever disease is attacking. When this is the case, we need strengthening. When I pray for the sick, I do not pray *to* the angels, but I do tell them, 'Do what you were assigned to do—go forth and strengthen and heal the people in Jesus' name.'

"I know from personal experience that angels do strengthen us. I had a particularly intense angelic visitation not too long ago. I was up all night talking with an angel, but I did not feel the least bit tired the next day. Alertness came to me. I really felt strengthened. In the presence of the angel, I felt plugged into something vital and alive.

"Angels love the Messiah, and they gathered to strengthen His earthly body and assist Him throughout His earthly life. When we love the Messiah, they operate in our lives. It is a powerful concept to realize that today, we believers *are* the Body of Messiah. They minister to us—the spiritually connected Body of Messiah—just as they ministered to His body on several occasions.

"Angels want to bring rest and strength to your life. Angels are here to help you work smarter, to take the weariness out of your life, and to add joy to it. Wherever I am, I am not alone. I am always happy and have a smile on my face."

## Angel Escorts

In the Bible we read that Elijah did not actually die, but that angels came to get him. (See Second Kings 2:1-11.) This is an important part of their service to believers even today. Ron has found that when believers are dying, they often see an angel coming for them. They die in peace and without fear.

"When I was a young preacher I went to visit an elderly retired Methodist pastor in the hospital. Although he was experiencing the last hours of his life, he was watching an angel in the corner. I looked and I also saw a faint light over there.

"The pastor told the nurses and his visitors that he was going home and that angels were there to take him home. In his last moments he had a joyful and peaceful expression, and seemed to just slip out of his body.

"As a pastor, I have been present at the going home of many believers. You cannot have fear if you see the angels coming for you, and children and those of strong faith are often able to see them. We should have grace and peace in death. We are not going to be alone. The angels are there to escort believers home. You are not going to be alone."

## Angelic Activity Is Increasing

Based on biblical examples and the experiences of modern-day believers, Ron is confident that angels are meant to partner with ordinary believers. "There is a tremendous increase in the number of angels making contact with people. Today, the majority of people you may ask will say they have experienced a life-saving intervention in their lives due to some hidden agent that they can't explain.

"For example, in my younger years, I was driving a car too fast and it hit a bridge abutment and flipped up into the air. The car landed and rolled over three times, and I was not wearing a seatbelt. It was a horrible wreck, but the whole time I felt that I was wrapped in a soft mattress, and I walked away from that wreck with no injury."

## Angels Serve the Heirs of Salvation

Hebrews 1:14 says that angels are sent to minister to those who are heirs of salvation. Ron has talked with hundreds of people who have now realized that they were helped by an angel. "For example, our friends, Coach Dubose and his wife Polly, had moved to Hattiesburg, Mississippi, with their young son. Polly had put the little boy to bed and was busy unpacking from the move. While Polly was unpacking, the little boy climbed out of his bed and went outside by himself. He got on his Big Wheel trike and went exploring in the neighborhood.

"Polly had no idea her son was in harm's way. She was continuing to unpack and put her house in order when the doorbell rang. At the door stood a stranger, a lady holding Polly's little boy. This stranger had found the child about two blocks away at a dangerous intersection, and had brought him home!

"Bear in mind that the Dubose family was new in town and did not know anyone in Hattiesburg. Polly took her son, then turned to thank the lady, but she was gone. Coach and Polly thanked God for sending an angel to rescue their son."

## How Do Angels Appear?

Many people wonder what angels look like, and whether they always have a physical manifestation. In the Scriptures they have appeared as men, with and without wings. They have also appeared as wind or fire and as spirits.

Ron says that angels can take any form that is necessary to perform their function; but if they manifest their presence, it is most often in a human form. Even when we cannot see their form, we can sense their presence or the effects of their actions.

This happened to a young mother from Ron's church. "Ginny was delivering some merchandise to her friend's house. She had just put it on the porch and had turned to walk back to her car, when she saw the family's Chow dog blocking her path, growling and snarling and threatening her. Her friend had warned her that the dog was vicious and had bitten family members, but the dog was supposed to be penned up in the back of the house.

"Ginny's first response was terror, but she became mindful of Scriptures that repeatedly said, *'Fear not!'* She had learned that fear and faith are mutually exclusive and cannot occupy the same heart at the same time. She declared aloud, 'I WILL NOT FEAR!' As quickly as the force swept over her, the dog retreated.

"Ginny responded with faith that God's angels watched over her (see Ps. 91) and were sent to minister to the heirs of salvation (see Heb. 1:14). So she spoke, 'Angels, I charge you in the name of Jesus to move this dog down the sidewalk, put him back in his fence and let me pass safely back to my car.'

"Next, Ginny saw an amazing thing. The animal got a stunned look in his eyes. His head was pressed down to the sidewalk as if an invisible hand had taken hold of his neck and he was pulled away from her by an invisible force until the dog turned himself and walked toward the back of the house. He never came at her again and she was able to safely return to her car.

"Ginny has no doubt that an angel came and helped her. What is important to note is that she received help, as I did, when she spoke to the angel. Angels do not read your mind. Angels move when the Word of God is voiced. They are not necessarily going to move until you speak. So when you need them, say to the angels, 'Get out there and help me!'"

## Angels Protect Us

Psalm 34:7 says, *"The angel of the Lord encamps all around those who fear Him, and delivers them."* Nowhere is the protective work of angels more beautifully laid out than in the 91st Psalm. This Psalm, sometimes called our covenant of protection, traces a pathway from *intimacy* with God to *overcoming* to *protection.*

## Psalm 91—Safety of Abiding in the Presence of God

> ¹*He who dwells in the secret place of the Most High shall abide under the shadow of the Almighty.*
>
> ²*I will say of the LORD, "He is my refuge and my fortress; my God, in Him I will trust."*
>
> ³*Surely He shall deliver you from the snare of the fowler and from the perilous pestilence.*
>
> ⁴*He shall cover you with His feathers, and under His wings you shall take refuge; His truth shall be your shield and buckler.*
>
> ⁵*You shall not be afraid of the terror by night, nor of the arrow that flies by day,*
>
> ⁶*Nor of the pestilence that walks in darkness, nor of the destruction that lays waste at noonday.*
>
> ⁷*A thousand may fall at your side, and ten thousand at your right hand; but it shall not come near you.*

<sup></sup>*⁸Only with your eyes shall you look, and see the reward of the wicked.*

*⁹Because you have made the LORD, who is my refuge, even the Most High, your dwelling place,*

*¹⁰No evil shall befall you, nor shall any plague come near your dwelling;*

*¹¹For He shall give His angels charge over you, to keep you in all your ways.*

*¹²In their hands they shall bear you up, lest you dash your foot against a stone.*

*¹³You shall tread upon the lion and the cobra, the young lion and the serpent you shall trample underfoot.*

*¹⁴"Because he has set his love upon Me, therefore I will deliver him; I will set him on high, because he has known My name.*

*¹⁵He shall call upon Me, and I will answer him; I will be with him in trouble; I will deliver him and honor him.*

*¹⁶With long life I will satisfy him, and show him My salvation."*

## Intimacy With God Is the Place of Safety

Ron explains: "In this Psalm, the secret place of the Most High is the place of intimacy with God. We are to abide in the shadow of the Almighty. The word *abide* means to tarry all night. It speaks of the intimacy of a husband and wife who tarry all night loving each other. If we are going to avoid evil, we must take time to have an intimate relationship with the Lord and to know our Maker in all His aspects.

"The words of the Psalm speak of safety and freedom from every kind of fear. It is the Holy of Holies experience. You are alone with God, and angels overshadow you.

"The secret to entering the intimacy of the Holy Place is praise. God inhabits the praises of His people. When we begin to confess His praises with our lips and to extol His might and power, then we have an open door into His presence."

In his book *Our Invisible Allies,* Ron explains this relationship in greater detail. "Intimacy with the Lord is the foundation. Angelic protection grows out of this trust and closeness with the Lord. When we abide in this place, Jesus and His angelic hosts step in for us to be our shield and protection."

## From Safety to Immunity

"As we read through Psalm 91, it is easy to see a progression from intimacy to protection to immunity. It is good to get healed, but it is even better if we never get sick, never fall. There is a place of such closeness to God that demonic forces cannot go there.

"God does give us seasons of rest from trials. The key is intimacy; everything begins with intimate worship. In verse 9 and 10, the psalmist says, *'Because you have made the Lord, who is my refuge, even the Most High, your dwelling place, no evil will befall you.'*

From studying Psalm 91 we can see that at the place of immunity, accidents do not happen, and sickness does not spread to your home. Angels will operate effectively to protect you, even to protecting you from tripping over a rock as it says in Psalm 91:12! You gain victory over your adversaries. Your protection is complete through the revealed promises. Our part is to dwell in His presence, love His name, and desire to know Him better.

"As we know Him better, His names become more meaningful to us. Some of His names are *Yahweh, the Great I Am; Jireh, my Provider;*

*Tsidkenu, my Righteousness; Rophe, my Healer; Rohi, my Shepherd; Nissi, my Leader and Lover; Shalom, my Peace and Shammah, my Companion."*[2]

## Angels Released in Worship

The Bible says that God is enthroned on the praises of His people. Ron has learned that angels are released in worship. Worship should be the foundation of the church service, not an afterthought.

"Worship is a sacred time in our church. Once we begin the worship part of our service, we do not allow interruptions, because we are paying honor to the Lord. We start with high praise—loud, vibrant music—and we enter into His gates with praise.

"Often this vibrant praise moves gradually from songs we know into worshipful singing in the Holy Spirit. The whole congregation will spontaneously begin to sing in the spirit. You cannot orchestrate melodies and rhythms that are as beautiful.

"Paul says I will sing with the understanding and I will sing in the spirit (see 1 Cor. 14:15). In Ephesians 5:19 he says, *'Speaking to one another in psalms, hymns, and spiritual songs, singing and making melody in your heart to the Lord.'"*

## Hearing the Angels Worship

"When we move beyond the melodies of the hymnbook, God introduces His music and rhythms to our hearts and our spirits. You will hear it like a Gregorian chant or like a wave moving across the congregation. At these times, God lets us tap into the music of the heavens. There is a majesty and beauty to this that is impossible to describe.

"Richard Ris's book on the Revival of 1948 describes a heavenly choir. In our worship times, many also have the sense of angels worshiping with us, beyond the congregation. It is an incomparably sweet sound with a flow and waves of tone after tone meeting each other. There is a sense of music and water running at the same time. One time I heard water flowing so clearly that I thought someone had turned on our baptismal pool, but it was the angels worshiping with us.

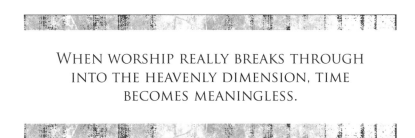

WHEN WORSHIP REALLY BREAKS THROUGH INTO THE HEAVENLY DIMENSION, TIME BECOMES MEANINGLESS.

"On a mission trip to Guatemala, we were worshiping and singing in the Spirit. We began to see orbs of light over peoples' heads. This also happened in Brazil. It was glorious. When worship really breaks through into the heavenly dimension, time becomes meaningless. Heaven is kissing earth and the dimensional boundaries are breached. This makes the supernatural possible. A dimensional interruption like this is ministered and served by angels."

## Ron's Angel of Joy

Perhaps it is because of Ron's church's dedication to worship that a special angel seems to show up in their services. Ron laughs when he talks about this special angel: "There is an angel who brings an anointing of joy. This angel is at every service in a particular spot, and people just get tickled when they are in that spot. I often have visitors sit there so they will leave feeling happy.

"One time we had four young ladies who were students from Lee University visit our church. I had them sit in the same corner where the joy angel stands because there is always happiness and joy that comes to people near him. One of the young ladies felt something touch her on the back, and then she immediately started laughing, something she was not used to doing in church. It was the joy angel. These young ladies later joined our church and have been very good, solid additions to our community.

"The presence of the joy angel is a sovereign thing that happened at our church. I wrote a book called *Awakened by the Spirit* that describes every awakening and every manifestation from the beginning of the church, because I don't think people realize how supernatural our faith is supposed to be."

## Faith Is Supposed to Be Supernatural

It took an awakening for Ron to realize that his faith was supposed to be supernatural. For many years, he had clung to his religious tradition. "Although the apostle Paul speaks of praying in the tongues of angels, for many years I did not understand this passage and objected to the idea of praying in tongues along with other supernatural manifestations. However, God had other plans.

"Twenty years ago, I had become a successful Southern Baptist pastor, but I was not seeing the level of change in peoples' lives that I thought I should see. There were occasions when I watched preachers like Oral Roberts, and so I knew there was more.

"I had gone to a conference in New Mexico on April 19, 1989. I heard a woman speak whose husband had recently died. She talked about how she had fallen into the arms of the Holy Spirit and felt refreshed. It stirred something in me that told me I needed to understand the full supernatural of God."

# God Spoke

Later that same night, Ron had an experience that gave him that supernatural connection. "I was in my bedroom about midnight and was sound asleep. I heard my name called audibly. I had been asleep, and the first time I just sort of woke up, but after the third time of hearing my name called, I was fully awake and I knew it was God. Just as Eli had told Samuel, I said, 'Speak, Lord, your servant is here.'

"The Lord told me plainly and in English, '*Read your Psalms for today.*' I got out of bed and read Psalm 91 about the protection of the secret place and then I read Psalm 92:10 that says, '*I have been anointed with fresh oil.*'

"I was pondering what this meant, when all of a sudden the fresh oil of the Holy Spirit fell on me. I began expressing my love to the Father in a fresh new way and lifted up my hands to God in praise. It hit me like a bolt of lightning, like an earthquake! I shook all over and then I lost awareness of my surroundings.

"My life has never been the same. My wife, Paulette, would wake me in the night telling me I was speaking in tongues. I used to preach against tongues, and immediately when I became conscious that I was actually doing it, I stopped and did not try to do it any more. God was blowing the roof off of my spiritual house.

"I was careful how I told people because I did not want to split my congregation by introducing this news. However, I believe in the inerrancy of Scripture, and when I realized it was scriptural, I accepted it. I am 62 years old now. I have only one regret: that I did not know all this earlier.

"After my experience in New Mexico, I had a much better ability to help people. It seemed that the anointing for the supernatural world opened up to me. The people I prayed for were really helped, and the miracles I saw in my ministry increased. I also found that praying in tongues was very restful and also helpful."

# Speaking in Tongues—a New Testament Church Practice

There is strong scriptural support for speaking in tongues. There are over a dozen references to speaking in tongues in the New Testament, and the writings of Paul make it clear that this was part of the ordinary practice of the early church.

*And these signs will follow those who believe: In My name they will cast out demons; they will speak with new tongues* (Mark 16:17).

*Then there appeared to them divided tongues, as of fire, and one sat upon each of them. And they were all filled with the Holy Spirit and began to speak with other tongues, as the Spirit gave them utterance* (Acts 2:3-4).

*And when Paul had laid hands on them, the Holy Spirit came upon them, and they spoke with tongues and prophesied* (Acts 19:6).

*I wish you all spoke with tongues, but even more that you prophesied; for he who prophesies is greater than he who speaks with tongues, unless indeed he interprets, that the church may receive edification* (1 Corinthians 14:5).

*Though I speak with the tongues of men and of angels, but have not love, I have become sounding brass or a clanging cymbal* (1 Corinthians 13:1).

Ron explains: "Paul says though he speaks with the tongues of men and angels—there are dialects of heavenly language. When we speak in faith, the angels show up. Tongues bring rest to your spirit.

"Every believer should be able to speak in tongues; it is a restful way to praise God and to pray. To receive your heavenly language, you just need to believe that you can speak with the tongues of men and of angels and move your lips. The utterance will come forth from your spirit. God is not going to manipulate your mouth—just do it yourself."

## An Angel Brings Peace

A particularly noble-looking angel has appeared to Ron and has become a frequent companion. "It was late one night, just after I had completed my book about angels, that I had a lengthy visitation from an angel. I was awakened by a large man-like figure with golden hair. He was so tall he had to bend his head to fit in the bedroom. He asked me to go down to my study and there he talked with me.

"My church and I had been through twenty years of criticism for accepting the full Gospel. I am a Bible scholar with a doctorate from seminary and I have studied Greek all my life. I have written several books, including one that documents supernatural manifestations in previous revival awakenings. Revival awakenings have revitalized the faith throughout the centuries. Nonetheless, I was under constant attack for teaching these things.

"The angel told me that he was going to defend my reputation and would grant me favor so that I would not be distracted by criticism and controversy. Then he said that together we were going to attack the occult and the spirits of witchcraft and domination. He had come to bring a season of favor, which I believe is happening."

## The Angels' Unemployment Problem

"Something I discovered is that angels move on miracle ground where Kingdom operation is going on. Hebrews 1:14 says that God has given the angels to be our servants, ministers for all those who are heirs of salvation.

"Human beings, before we come to the Messiah, are a little lower than the angels. When we come to the Messiah, we move from that 'human' realm to being a joint heir with Jesus. At that moment, the same angels who strengthened Him when He was in His earthly body now come to strengthen His new Body, which is made up of all those who believe in Him."

## Guiding Principles

Angels are standing near, ready to flood and invade your home right now, but there are important things that you need to know. Particularly, you need to know that you matter. You are important to God's plans and angels are standing by, waiting for you to call on them for help. Some of the guiding principles that Ron has identified are:

1. **Faith**—Angels are activated by faith. The angel went before the Hebrews as they left Egypt because they believed they were going somewhere. Study the Scriptures about angels, and let your faith go forth on this.

2. **Words**—Nothing is stronger than the declared Word of God. Angels immediately respond to the obedient, repentant believer who speaks forth the promises of God. You need to be careful about what comes out of your mouth and recognize that the words you speak are being heard by the angels.

3. **Prayer**—We do not pray to angels. We pray to God our heavenly Father, and the angels convey our prayers in their hands to Him (see Rev. 5 and 8). The promises of God are released to those who live in prayerful intimacy with Him.

4. **Praise and Worship**—Draw close to your Father through praise and worship. Since our body is the temple of the Holy Spirit, when the Word and worship and prayer begin to roll out of our

spirit, it is like when Isaiah was in the Holy of Holies. There is no veil between us.

5. **Love**—Angels are stirred by the love of God. It is vitally important to realize that every man and woman of God has angels about them, and the angels are connected to each other in ways we can't begin to understand. When you speak against a man or woman of God, you are creating a disturbance and confusion in the heavenly realms. You really limit your angel's ability to help you because of sowing confusion and distress. Angels work in community.

6. **Helping Others**—There is a connection between walking in love and having angelic help. When we walk in love and an attitude of service, angelic activity increases. When you help someone in need, angelic activity and strength around you increases. Angelic favor can be released on us in a moment.

\* \* \*

To learn more about the ministry of angels, read Ron Phillips' book, *Our Invisible Allies*. For more information about Pastor Ron Phillips and his ministry, visit his Website at www.ronphillips.org.

# Endnotes

1. Ron Phillips, *Our Invisible Allies* (Lake Mary, FL: Charisma House, 2009), 22. Used with permission.

2. Ibid., 92-98.

Chapter 4

# A Heart in Unity
# With God's Heart

## Michael Hinson

*Keep your heart with all diligence; for out of it*
*spring the issues of life* (Proverbs 4:23).

Michael Hinson has served in the healing ministry most of his life, often witnessing dramatic miracles. "After years in ministry," he says, "the most important thing I can pass on to others is that the Kingdom of Heaven lives within our hearts! We can only see it with our hearts. When we get our hearts in unity with God's heart, we can experience and live in a reality that cannot be seen with natural eyes. This reality is greater and more amazing than anything you can imagine."

Michael has endless stories of people he has seen healed: "In one meeting a 10-year-old boy came up for prayer who had a leg brace on one leg from his knee to the floor due to an undeveloped leg. His leg was at least a full foot shorter, and yet that little boy left the meeting carrying his leg brace. Both legs were the exact same length, and he was completely healed.

"On another occasion, I prayed for a baby girl with a tumor who had been given no hope. When the parents took her back to the doctor, he wanted to know what they did, because the tumor was gone!

"I remember the first blind woman I prayed for. She had lost her sight through an irreversible disease of the retina. I laid hands on her eyes and pressed hard because I desperately wanted to see her healed. When this lady told me she was seeing flashes of light, my first thought was that I had pressed too hard on her eyes. However, when I prayed a second time, she told me she could see people like shadows. So I prayed a third time, and when I took my hands off her eyes, she could see so well that she picked up my Bible and started reading it.

"My experience has been that healing is easy when you understand it is a natural part of the Kingdom of God, much like breathing."

## God Lives Within Us

"We were made in God's image, so much so that we resemble Him. He is the blueprint to our life here on earth and our life in the future. The more we know of Him, the more we know about ourselves.

"Many of us do not know who God is from firsthand experience. We only know about Him what others have told us. We make assumptions, and try to fit God into our belief system. We might even apply to Him the characteristics we believe He *should* have. In other words, if we do not know God for who He really is, we will tend to believe that God is *like us!* We reduce God to being like us instead of rising to the call of becoming like Him.

"God is not who our traditions say He is. When we see the truth of who God is, we know how much good He desires for us, and healing comes very naturally. I have seen this proven time and again in my ministry."

## Truth Brings Healing

"Recently I was at a farm visiting a family that trains horses. The husband was having a difficult time working with the horses because he had a very bad back and his wife asked me to help him. I told him, 'There is something more going on here than your back. You need to have a change of heart.' I suggested he stop all of his complaining, moaning, and groaning and take the time to learn to be thankful.

"I even suggested that should he catch himself complaining again, he should stop and give thanks for at least three things, no matter how small. This man was suddenly struck with the truth of what I said. He repented for his negative attitude and was immediately healed. His back was just manifesting the condition of his heart. When we see the truth as it really is, we are set free and made whole."

## God's Love Touched My Heart

"Apart from miracles, healing the heart is usually the key to healing the body. However, most people don't realize their hearts may need healing. This was true of me at one time. I did not imagine that my heart was dark.

"I thought I was living for God and loved my family. I worked full time in ministry, and I frequently saw sudden miracles such as blind eyes being opened and cancers vanishing. However, it did not happen often enough for me, so I prayed constantly to God, asking Him for something more.

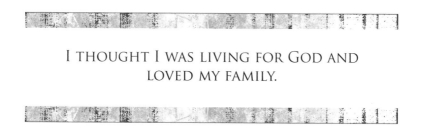

I THOUGHT I WAS LIVING FOR GOD AND
LOVED MY FAMILY.

"In answer to this prayer, God gave me a three-day-long revelation of the Messiah. It was not a dream. I was physically in His presence, and I was allowed to experience the complete selflessness and purity of Jesus' nature. In my prayer—for something more—I was hoping to be overwhelmed by the joy of His love and presence. But I was not prepared for what happened. Instead of joy, I experienced the fear of God's judgment."

## The Darkness Within Me Was Frightening

"This fear came when I was allowed to see myself in the presence of Jesus' glory. His glory radiated as an intense bright light that came from every direction and totally exposed my heart. My whole life was laid out before me—everything I had ever done, every word I had ever spoken. All that was down in my consciousness was revealed.

"I had once thought that at the time for judgment my life would unfold like one would watch a movie. Instead, everything in me that did not reflect the light that came from Him was exposed as darkness inside of me, and the source of that darkness was instantly known to all.

"I was shocked and saddened at what I saw in myself. I had believed that I was a good person and that my life was dedicated to God's service. However, in the pure light of His presence, I saw that all my good motives and good intentions were utterly, utterly darkness.

"What I saw in myself was so dark that I could hardly bear to be in His presence. There were moments when I was so horrified and so devastated, that I am sure I would have died if He had not had mercy on me and slowed the process of revelation."

## Jesus Did Not Condemn Me

"Jesus did not condemn me. It was the darkness *in* me that was condemning. As I was experiencing all of this, I was keenly aware of His intense love and I knew He only wanted me to reflect the light that shone from Him. That is what He wants for all of us.

"There was so much more that happened during that time, it would take weeks to explain it all. It suffices to say that during those three days, I gained an understanding of God's heart that changed me profoundly."

## My Heart Was Transformed

"After this encounter the people in my life noticed an immediate change. I repented for selfishness and my hardness of heart. My desire became that of reflecting God's love through caring for others. I have a heartfelt love, even for strangers, that can't be explained in words.

"My family and friends were astonished at the way His love and compassion began to flow out of me. I had always tried to be loving and kind before this experience, but now it was different. Before I felt a need to love people and help them be better than they already are, but now I love people just as they are.

"I had no idea a heart could hold so many people in it. Don't misunderstand, I literally hurt for those who are lost or in dark places, and burn with the desire to see them set free from the oppressive lies they believe about themselves, but my love for them is independent of their condition."

## Love God by Loving Others

"Jesus showed me that with the measure that we love others, we love Him. The way we love others is the visual text of the love of God in our lives. We may profess to love God, but most often the concentration is on our own relationship with God. Concern for our brothers and sisters tends to come in second.

"But when we have His heart, we can't help but feel what He feels, to love what He loves as well as to hate what He hates, sharing His passions. Then our concern for our brothers and sisters is equal to our concern for ourselves. When we love others, we love God. We cannot separate the two although there is a difference. The heart cannot draw a line between the two."

## Loving Is Easy

"God is pure love. Those who know Him reflect His goodness into the world. Reflecting God's nature into the world around us is a by-product of that relationship. It comes naturally and is not hard work. If you have to work at it then you may believe some things about God's nature that are not the truth.

"But what if what you know about God is not correct? How would you know? What if you have been told from childhood that the color ivory is white? You would believe ivory to be white from that point on. This is best illustrated by the story about two brothers who shared the same room while they were growing up. The younger brother had been blind from birth, and when the older brother turned ten, he was given the responsibility to make sure his younger brother was properly dressed each day. One day, thinking he was being funny, he told his younger brother there was a right sock and left sock. Further amusing himself, he often told his brother he had his socks on the wrong foot. Years later, it took two roommates in college almost a month to convince the younger brother that he had believed something that was not true.

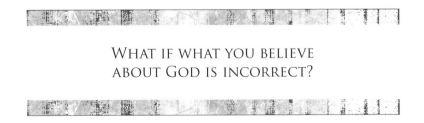

WHAT IF WHAT YOU BELIEVE
ABOUT GOD IS INCORRECT?

"So what if what you believe about God is incorrect...how would you know? You can tell by the quality and fruitfulness of your life. The fruit that I'm speaking of is love, peace, joy, and contentment. If you do not have these things consistently in your life, or know in your heart that something is missing, then you may believe some things about God that are not accurate. You may believe that something is ivory when God is speaking to you of white.

"What if this life full of fruit is as easy to obtain as changing the channel on your television set? Have you ever watched a program on television and found it unsatisfying and then changed the channel? The life I am talking about is as easy to obtain as that...switching channels."

## There Must Be Something More

"It is at this point that I lose the attention of most people because they are not new to the concept of contentment. Many have done everything they know to gain love, peace, joy, and a satisfying life. They have worked so hard at it that most have just settled for the belief that it is unobtainable.

"Some believe that there must be something wrong with them that must need to be fixed so that they can achieve this kind of life. So they pursue fixing the problems in their lives to achieve their goal. Although this may seem like the best way to get there—fix the broken areas of your life—it is not the answer. People with this belief spend a lifetime fixing themselves with only sporadic moments of satisfaction.

"There are those who find pursuits and escapes to deal with the emptiness or lack of love, peace, joy, and contentment. The extremes of this case are recognized as workaholics, alcoholics, and the like. However, a milder form of the same problem are people who consistently daydream of a better life or lose themselves in activities such as hobbies, sports, or television to find fulfillment. There is nothing wrong with these things, but when they are used as an escape it is only a temporary fix so you need to re-peat it. These people would not admit to this, but the signs are obvious.

"There are some who live their lives through other people. They be-lieve that if they could only find the right spouse or at least fix this one, then they could find love, peace, joy, and contentment. There are some parents who live their lives through their adult children by carrying their children's fears, concerns, and problems. Others even take control of their adult children's lives, hoping to find fulfillment through them.

"I could spend all my time talking about the errors made pursuing contentment, but you already know most of them, not to mention reli-gion. There are those who believe that they are just one step away from finding the fruit they are lacking through religion. They may believe that if they just prayed more, or read their Bible more, or gave more, or wor-shiped more, or fasted or...you can fill in the blank. There is absolutely nothing wrong with these things and they should all be practiced as your heart leads.

"However, none of these things in themselves is the answer to living a life of peace, love, joy, and contentment. I know this by experience. I meet believers every day who are in pursuit of this fruit because they have tasted it and believe they are only one step away from attaining it. This is something they have believed since the beginning of their walk with God. All of this pursuit is hard work and ultimately only yields frustration.

"Before you can change the channel in your life, the first thing that has to happen is to recognize the ivory in your life so you can see white. So let's take a look."

## Unforgiveness Is Poison

"Unforgiveness affects the whole body through tension, anxiety, de-pression, anger, and bitterness. It does not reflect God's nature. Harboring unforgiveness is like drinking poison, hoping the other person will get sick.

"God's declared Word says that we are forgiven in the measure that we forgive others. If we have unforgiveness in our heart, any indebtedness that we hold against another person will appear as darkness in us. Forgiving stops the poison and healing begins in a very natural way.

"At this point, you may be thinking, 'The people who sinned against me did not ask for forgiveness, so I don't have to forgive them.' It is important to point out that your forgiveness does not release them from their responsibility to God for their actions. However, it does release them from their responsibility to you for their debt."

## How to Forgive

"To make this easier, you may need to understand that you do not need to forgive what the other person did to you. Their actions were most likely sin. However, you *need to forgive the person* who sinned against you. Forgiving them won't do anything for them, but it will change everything for you. Release them from the debt they owe you—what you want them to do or have done to make it right.

"Some people don't know that they harbor unforgiveness. You should ask yourself if there is anyone in your past or in your present who makes you uncomfortable. Then ask yourself why. The answer may be that you have some unacknowledged unforgiveness.

"Forgiveness is not difficult when we understand it in its biblical context. In the Old Testament, when people sought forgiveness, they took an unblemished animal to the priest. Their sins were laid on the animal, and then the animal was killed.

"This was done because the Bible states that *'the wages of sin is death'* (see Rom. 6:23). The natural consequence of sin is death. In order to not have to suffer the consequences of our sinful actions, something or someone had to die in our stead.

"When a sacrifice was made, God was not saying that the person's sin was OK. What He did was separate the sin from the person. He pulled the sins away from people, placed it on the sacrificial animal, and He chose to remember the sins no more.

"This is a foreshadowing of Jesus on the cross. Jesus takes our sins onto Himself, all of the curse of the Law, and bears the punishment on our behalf. God has not condoned our sin, He has separated us from it by laying it on Jesus. He does not forget, but actively chooses to remember our sins no more because they are no longer part of us. He looks on us as clean in His sight, His Light. This is what it means to be forgiven.

"If you have unforgiveness toward anyone, then repeat this prayer:

*Father, what this person did to me was sin. In the name of Jesus the Messiah, take this sin from them and put it on the cross of Jesus. Separate it from them forever. Forgive them; and on the Day of Judgment when I stand before your throne, I will hold no accusation against them. They will be free. Even now I release them in Jesus' name. Father, bless them in every way possible and prosper them in Jesus' name.*

"This prayer activates power in the Spirit. When we live in the nature and character of God, the things of God become part of who we are. Our life changes and the things around us change as well.

"When you pray this in sincerity, you will be able to sense the tangible, sweet presence of God. There is a supernatural release of God's presence through forgiveness."

## Forgiveness Can Bring Instant Healing

"When people truly forgive, healing is often instantaneous; it is so easy that it is amazing. People say, 'I can't believe this joy is possible. I had no idea; I never imagined this. I have never felt such peace before in my life.'

"I remember a woman who was in constant, severe back pain and needed help to walk or sit down. She had received many prayers and tried many different medical treatments, but nothing had made a difference.

"She was so tired and worn looking that she appeared much older than her years. In the past, her husband had left her for his secretary, hurting her very deeply. Acrimony from the divorce had severely damaged relationships with her children, leaving her very lonely. This woman needed to forgive. The bitterness of that divorce was killing her.

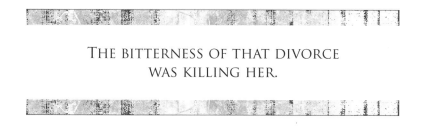

THE BITTERNESS OF THAT DIVORCE
WAS KILLING HER.

"I led her through a simple prayer of forgiveness in which she separated the sin from her husband, forgiving *him,* not what he did, and placed it on the cross. She truly extended forgiveness to him; I could tell she meant it. She cried for a few moments, then she stopped and looked up at me with such a beautiful expression. Her countenance had changed so much that she actually looked ten years younger!

"Joy had flooded her heart and healed her body. She leaped out of the chair, and began jumping up and down, excited to be pain free for the first time in years. Today she is still free of back pain. She is reconciled with her children and is content with her life."

## Healed of Chronic Fatigue Syndrome

"Mary was a faithful church member, but she suffered from depression, chronic fatigue syndrome, and fibromyalgia. Mary kept busy taking care of her family, but she had an emptiness inside her that was reflected in an emotionally distant relationship with her husband. Like many, Mary felt doomed to go through the motions of life looking for something more but never finding it.

"Mary's problem was that she had been hurt and had built a wall around her heart to protect herself from emotional pain. That wall had become a prison that trapped her in loneliness and depression. When she understood that the wall to protect herself separated her from the very people she wanted to share her heart with, she repented. As the wall broke down, a sense of joy washed over her, and all the symptoms left. She was completely healed and remains healed many years later, loving those from whom she was once alienated."

## Forgiveness Heals Marriages

"Our natural state is to love deeply, to give our hearts and be emotionally open, but hurt causes us to put up walls. We think that these walls will protect us, but they end up making us prisoners of loneliness and despair. Intimacy disappears and life loses its joy. So many people are just going through the motions of life.

"Many love God and love their spouse but have lost the sense of vulnerability and intimacy, even though they still love each other. This is not as it should be. I remember one lady in particular, let's call her Jane, who said she had lost that first love she used to feel toward her husband. She wanted to give her husband her heart but could not. She had put walls around her heart, and had many, many complaints about her husband's behavior.

"Jesus told people who were like this that they were no different from the tax collectors (see Matt. 5:46). This was not a compliment. The tax collectors would sit at the entrances, gates, around the wall of Jerusalem to collect the taxes due to Caesar. In that day, you were not allowed into the city unless your debt was paid. You could not trade your goods or worship at the temple until all your debt was paid.

"Some of us have put up a wall around our hearts, and we refuse to let people pass that wall until they pay the debt we feel they owe us. If this is you, then you are no different from the tax collectors. You are not living within God's nature, and your heart is hurting. You feel a loss of intimacy in your relationship with God and with others. The good news is that you do not have to stay in this condition.

"Jane knew that her heart was not completely open to her husband. She wanted to give him her heart, but fearing that he would hurt her again, she held it back. She felt trapped, with her only hope being that he might change. She even had a checklist of things he would have to do before she would open her heart to him again.

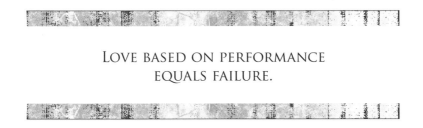

## LOVE BASED ON PERFORMANCE EQUALS FAILURE.

"I asked her if he did everything on the list would she give her heart back instantly or would she want to wait awhile to see if it 'took'? She said she would wait. Then I asked her if she had compiled a list and waited awhile for him to perform it the *first* time she gave her heart to him. You see, love based on performance equals failure.

"When she recognized the truth in this, she repented. I led her in this prayer: 'I (her name) give 100 percent of my heart to (husband's name) right now.'

"Almost immediately she said, 'I feel so good! I feel complete peace.' I could see the change. Her face looked younger, she laughed, she was happy. It was not just a passing emotional experience.

"A couple of months later, I talked to her, and her marriage had changed. She thought her husband had equally changed. She was surprised at the change that occurred in such a short period of time and all she did was give her heart back to her husband. She said, 'This is so easy.' And it is so easy.

"People often ask how such change can be so easy. It is just a matter of knowing the truth. When a person's heart motivation is to be free, they will recognize the truth. God will meet us at our heart level. People whose hearts are to find the truth will never be denied."

## Change the Channel and Find Love

"I recently received an email from a woman who had serious marital problems. She had gone to counseling regarding some serious issues. It was a volatile situation, an unhappy marriage with a lot of emotional pain.

"She had read my book and had repeated the prayers that I suggested, and something miraculous happened. She realized that she had been trying to concentrate on fixing her marriage and husband to achieve the perfect marriage, instead of enjoying what she had and what she needed to do to get the most out of life. Then she changed the channel. Things her husband did that would hurt her no longer bothered her as they did before. She wrote me that she had never comprehended how happy she could be."

## The Joy of the Lord Is Our Strength

"Many people put themselves under a great deal of stress, which can be a factor in illness. Often this arises from a misunderstanding of who God is and what He wants. What He wants is for us to be filled with His joy and to be led by His Spirit.

"Enjoying life is a celebration of the Lord and the life He gave us. Everything else is a lie. Jesus paid the price for us, and experiencing His joy is one way we can worship and thank Him. When we put our attention on being happy in the Lord, we can live life to the fullest and live it as a celebration unto God.

"The more you have intimacy with your Creator, the more your life becomes full. Fear of failure and fear of not doing it right disappears. Love can fill you to the point that you experience God's love in everyone you encounter. Your heart can love so many people—everyone you meet. Jesus loved everyone. It is really possible."

## Your Identity Is in God

"Many of us, especially men, get our identity from things we do, our jobs, and our possessions. We need to pick up our identity in God. We came from God's stock. He made us in His image, so that is where we must gain our identity.

"It is not what you *do* for God, it is who you are *in* God. Everything that is in our lives is there so that we can believe in God and be who we are in God. We are not here to accomplish things but to be accomplished in who we are in God. It is wonderful to make Jesus your Messiah and Lord. You are not a mistake. You have not missed it. There is a destiny for you."

## Freedom From Stress and Anxiety

"When I released forgiveness and compassion in my life, I became free and contentment now floods my soul. Worry has gone out the door of my life, and I live in a state of supernatural peace. Problems still arise, but they get taken care of in ways that are supernatural.

"Walking with God is easy. If it is complicated, if you are carrying burdens, worries, fear, and doubt, if you have sleeplessness or anxiety, the answers are simple—hope is on the way by repeating this prayer.

*Father I give you my anxieties, fears, and worries. I lay them down at the cross of Jesus the Messiah. I put them on Your altar and I give them to You. Father, those concerns in my heart and burdens that are not mine to carry, I give them to You. Father, I desire intimacy with You, and want Your love to fill my heart. I ask You to reach me and teach me. I will follow You in the name of Jesus the Messiah. I choose to surrender in Jesus' name, Amen.*

## What You Can Do

"Proverbs says, *'Keep your heart with all diligence; for out of it spring the issues of life'* (Prov. 4:23). God lives in our hearts and we can learn to hear His voice. We can trust our hearts to guide us and be led by our hearts in everything. We will have joy and peace and will be extremely productive. We can do so much—accomplish so much—in the joy of the Lord.

"We can live to fulfill the desire in our hearts that pleases God. An example would be the time I stopped a guy I had never met who was walking by me on the street. I simply told him that he would be OK. Something in my heart led me to do this. He started crying and thanked me over and over again. Following the leading of your heart will feed it as well as nourish the hearts of others.

"Another way to feed the heart is by God's written Word. I see it as reading love letters from the Lord. There is nothing in the Bible that the heart cannot explain—no mystery.

"When our hearts are submitted to God, we will recognize inner signals and repent when we do wrong—He wrote His laws on our hearts. There is no lasting guilt or shame. We learn by listening to our hearts and making mistakes. We can learn that we have overdone something by a sensitive heart and keeping ourselves teachable.

"Every day is a new day, and every day presents a brand-new opportunity to enjoy life. You are here for a reason; you have a destiny and a purpose in God, and He loves you."

* * *

More guidance for inner healing can be found in Michael's book *To Heal the Heart and Live Life to the Fullest*. For more information about Michael Hinson and his ministry, visit his Website at www.hinsonministries.com.

# Chapter 5

# Freedom From Toxic Emotions
## *Dr. Art Mathias*

*Understanding is a wellspring of life...* (Proverbs 16:22).

Many have noted that forgiveness is an important pathway to supernatural healing. Dr. Art Mathias is living proof that when we understand and apply the principles of biblical forgiveness, toxic emotions are released and the Lord's healing will often come to us very easily. His simple approach has set thousands free from suffering and disability, including blind and deaf persons who have experienced creative miracles.

Art discovered these principles as part of his own healing journey. Faced with a terminal illness, he searched the Bible for Scriptures about healing. Over and over again he saw Scriptures that connected physical conditions in the body with spiritual health.

He saw that repentance and forgiveness are closely connected to physical healing, and learned that even subtle sins such as resentment, shame, and worry give the devil a way to attack our health, and can block the flow of the Lord's healing power.

When he applied simple principles found in the Bible, Art was completely healed. These principles have formed the basis for Wellspring Ministries, a ministry that has brought healing to many from almost every kind of mental and physical disorder. The following describes Art's path to finding the wellsprings of life.

## Two Years to Live

In February 1997, Art Mathias sustained a neck injury, and by the fall of that year, the pain had progressed and his arm had withered. He had surgery that fused four levels in his neck to alleviate the symptoms, but he developed some unexpected complications.

Art describes what happened: "Following surgery to repair my neck injury, I suddenly became allergic to almost everything. I could only eat four foods, and it hurt to eat even those foods. My skin grew so sensitive that it hurt to put on clothing.

"The nerves in my toes and fingers burned, then grew numb and were dying. The numbness was progressing up my arms and legs. I went to the Mayo Clinic in Scottsdale, Arizona, where doctors diagnosed this disorder as *small fiber neuropathy*. They told me that the neuropathy would progress until it reached a vital organ, and estimated I had two years to live before it killed me."

Art asked his church elders to pray for him. In addition, he tried many different medical treatments and a great many alternative treatments, but nothing stopped the progress of the neuropathy.

Art says, "The pain was horrible, but even worse was my level of fear. Something I did not understand and could not stop was slowly killing me. But God had a plan! At just about the darkest hour of my life, my sister was supernaturally healed of breast tumors. She explained that she had gone to a divine healing seminar, and that when she got rid of buried resentments in her heart, the tumors just disappeared. She recommended that I try it.

I WAS SO DESPERATE THAT I DECIDED TO
SEARCH THE BIBLE AND SEE WHAT IT
SAID ABOUT HEALTH.

"I was quite skeptical for several reasons. In the first place, I had been a Christian all my life, even gone to a Christian college and majored in Bible Studies, and not only had I not heard of being healed by forgiveness, I did not think I had any sins bad enough to kill me. In the second place, I believed, as do many, that we received total forgiveness when we accepted the Messiah as our Savior. So I thought that whatever sins I did have were covered by the blood of Jesus. However, I was so desperate that I decided to search the Bible and see what it said about health."

## Our Bodies Reflect Our Spiritual Health

"The Bible actually teaches that our bodies are barometers for what is going on spiritually in our lives. There are many, many passages, particularly in the Book of Proverbs, that point to the spirit-body relationship.

"One passage in particular that meant a lot to me is Third John 1:2: *'Beloved, I pray that you may prosper in all things and be in health, just as your soul prospers.'* Our health will prosper even as our soul prospers.

"My health really did begin to prosper when I discovered Hebrews 12:12-15:

*Therefore strengthen the hands which hang down, and the feeble knees, and make straight paths for your feet, so that what is lame may not be dislocated, but rather be healed. Pursue peace with all people, and holiness, without which no one will see the Lord:*

*looking carefully lest anyone fall short of the grace of God; lest any root of bitterness springing up cause trouble, and by this many become defiled* (Hebrews 12:12–15).

"I could see a very plain warning to beware of any root of bitterness, meaning beware of buried resentment or hurt. Bitterness of any kind defiles our souls, and directly affects our bodies."

## The Truth Set Me Free

"Roots of bitterness can be buried deep inside us. If we don't dig them out, we risk missing the grace of God. In my heart I knew that this was the truth I needed to be healed. With the direction of the Holy Spirit, I looked diligently inside myself and confronted my own buried resentments, forgotten offenses, and deep-seated fears.

"I began to work through all my memories as the Holy Spirit brought them to my mind. For each one, I asked God to forgive me and to forgive others who had hurt or offended me. Although I have since learned that there is a little more to it, God honored the intent of my heart, and I immediately began to feel better."

## Battling Against Spiritual Powers

"I was not totally restored, however, so I kept searching the Scriptures. What I next uncovered was the importance of satan's power against us.

*We do not war against flesh and blood but against principalities, against powers, against the rulers of the darkness of this age, and against spiritual hosts of wickedness in heavenly places* (Ephesians 6:12).

"Although I knew that Jesus cast demon spirits out of many, including a spirit of infirmity, I had always believed that Christians could not be troubled by evil spirits. However, I did know that I was controlled by fear of the future due to my illness.

"I also remembered that Paul referred to a spirit of fear in Second Timothy 1:7, and that James 4:7 advises to *'resist the devil and he shall flee from you.'* I realized that I really did have to battle the devil to obtain my healing."

## I Was Completely Healed

"I wanted to be completely free of bitterness before I confronted the devil. By January 1999, I had completed the work of forgiving all my past hurts and resentments, so I was ready to do this.

"I cancelled all of satan's assignments against me, and commanded the spirit of fear to leave in the name of Jesus. Amazingly, the fear left instantly and all the allergies and neuropathies went with it.

*"I was totally healed!* God healed my nerve damage, restored my right arm and shoulder completely, and healed all my allergies. My health was completely restored!"

## Others Wanted Healing Help

"People who knew me were astonished. They had known how sick I was. Now they could see my glowing good health, and they wanted me to pray for them. I began to work with these friends individually. Word spread quickly to others because the results were so plainly visible. People were getting healed as they learned how to repent and forgive themselves as well as the people in their lives who had hurt or offended them.

"I started teaching classes and training others to bring healing through forgiveness. We quickly realized that the same principles apply whatever the toxic emotion might be. Gradually we grew into a large ministry that now serves thousands of people a year through direct counseling, outreach ministry, and classes. We named our ministry Wellspring Ministries because *'Understanding is a wellspring of life'* (Prov. 16:22)."

## Repentance and Forgiveness— Important Healing Keys

"We have documented results of almost every kind of disease being healed with this approach, including lupus, multiple sclerosis, cancer, heart disease, autism, mental illness, addictions, hepatitis C, chronic fatigue syndrome, and fibromyalgia. We have seen creative miracles that include sight being restored to the blind and deaf people receiving their hearing.

*"There is nothing that cannot be healed when we get our hearts right with God.* Seventy-five percent of people who come to our ministry are completely healed. Usually we know why someone is not healed, but sometimes a person will do everything that we ask, but the healing still does not happen. We are asking God for more answers, because we firmly believe that it is always His will to heal. There is no disease, no condition, and no disorder that resists the healing power of God when we get rid of our inner fears, resentments, and hurts. *Repentance and forgiveness are the keys.*

"When I go different places and teach this truth, many in the audiences receive healing while they sit there—just as they release their own bitterness. For example, a man had lost his sight when a hydraulic hose broke, spraying his eyes with caustic fluid. He received his vision back completely. Another man ended a lifetime of severe migraine headaches when he released buried feelings about his son's death. Over twenty people have received healing from deafness and eight from blindness. There is nothing that God cannot heal if we will only be obedient and forgive, releasing our hurts, resentments, fears, guilt, and shame. God wants us to be well, but we must do our part."

## Our Part to Play

"Sin separates us from God. Even the inward thoughts of our hearts can be sin if they reflect unforgiveness or hurt. Every year thousands die of heart disease because deep inside, their hearts were broken because someone deeply hurt them.

"Another major block to healing is a tendency to blame God for the disease or believe that He somehow inflicted it. God is good, and He only gives good and perfect gifts. It is important to understand that all disease is from the devil.

"We allow disease ourselves when we are disobedient to God's Word. As mentioned previously, in Third John 1:2 we read, *'Beloved, I wish above all things that you might prosper and be in health, **even as your soul prospers.'***

"This verse says that God wants us to be healthy, but our soul must also be doing well, and be free of sin. Sin, even if it is hidden or subtle, can separate us from the promises of God. Our job is to unearth every sin or bitterness and root it out of our lives."

## Four Steps to Healing

"The Bible is clear that God wants to heal all our infirmities, whether mental, emotional, or physical. However, we have a part to play. We must be obedient and get the sin, unforgiveness and hurt out of our lives so that the power of God is free to flow. If we are not obedient, there will be blockages to the flow of God's power. Dealing with our own toxic emotions through repentance and forgiveness is the first step.

"We must also cancel satan's assignment against us. By allowing even small sins in our lives, we have inadvertently given the devil the right to afflict us with various kinds of problems. Ephesians 4:27 tells us not to give a place, room, or right to the devil. We do this by disobeying God.

"So we must actually tell the symptoms to leave us, and refuse to let them come back. Once these two steps are completed, the third step is to ask the Holy Spirit to come and bring comfort and healing. The process is complete with a fourth step—asking the Holy Spirit to show us God's truth about the situation.

"This is a simple, biblical approach to healing. I have seen it work in over 75 percent of the thousands who have come to our ministry with physical or emotional disorders."

## The Effects of Toxic Emotions

Recent research has suggested a possible scientific explanation for the close connections between toxic emotions and illness. Everyone has experienced the way the body reacts to stress. Stress causes adrenalin to spike each time we become emotional. When adrenalin spikes, the muscles tense, the heart rate increases and digestion stops. There are over 1,400 different chemical and neuro-hormonal responses that occur during emotional stress.

These reactions make up the "fight or flight response"—our inborn survival reaction. It is what enables us to run away from danger or confront problem situations. The fight or flight response is activated to the greatest degree during panic states and rage reactions, and to a lesser degree when we experience ordinary fear and anger in daily life.

Recently researchers have found that it is even activated when we experience milder emotions such as worry, anxiety, frustration, or resentment. Toxic emotions have been scientifically proven through hundreds of studies to affect our bodily processes.[1]

## Bitterness Creates Illness

Every emotion produces numerous chemical changes in the body, whether we are aware of it or not. Living in a state of fight or flight activation caused by anxiety, resentment, or shame, puts significant stress on our bodies and creates the biochemical basis for disease.

Art explains, "In my case, resentment and unforgiveness had caused my body to produce too much adrenaline, which had weakened my immune system—thus allowing the allergies and neuropathy. This was causing my nerve endings to die, to the point that the doctors believed the process would cause my death within two years. *The bitterness I held inside could have actually killed me.*

"When we deal with our emotional pain, we get rid of the bitter root that causes stress (see Heb. 12:15). God's peace flows in, and our bodies function in homeostasis as God intended. Stress reactions stop and the body heals. We really can have supernatural true peace through the Messiah."

## Self-Bitterness and Illness

"In our ministry we see many whose diseases stem from self-bitterness, which is unforgiveness and judgments that we hold against ourselves. Self-bitterness includes feelings of shame and guilt, regret and sorrows, perfectionism and the general put-downs we do to ourselves. The devil destroys us and deprives us of God's promises by convincing us that certain lies about ourselves are true. Those lies are things such as 'I am unattractive. I'm a failure. I will never feel love. I am a laughingstock. I am no good to anyone.'

"Through our normal experiences, we can come to believe the lies of the devil about ourselves, not the truth that we are God's beloved children. It is important to release this self-bitterness and learn who we really are as spiritual beings.

"In Matthew 22:39, Jesus says, *'Love your neighbor as yourself.'* **The second greatest commandment contains the instruction to love ourselves.** Many of us have to re-learn the truth that we are created in God's image, and that He loves us unconditionally. As we accept forgiveness for ourselves, we gain self-respect, releasing God's healing power to flow within us.

"Almost all autoimmune diseases are in some way related to self-bitterness. In self-bitterness, there is a deep-seated condemnation of the self, basically putting the person at war with him or herself. This continuing internal stress results in a low level fight or flight response that taxes the internal organ systems.

"A good example of this is Type 2 diabetes, a disease that involves the pancreas and afflicts 23 percent of Americans. As noted, during stress the body increases the supply of energy available by increasing the level of glucose (sugar) in the blood. When the muscles fail to use this glucose, the pancreas reacts to high levels of blood sugar by secreting insulin to lock it up.

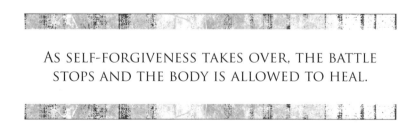

AS SELF-FORGIVENESS TAKES OVER, THE BATTLE
STOPS AND THE BODY IS ALLOWED TO HEAL.

"In diabetes the body is in a constant battle between the liver putting out sugar and the pancreas locking it up, with the body eventually becoming resistant to insulin and the pancreas simply wearing out. As self-forgiveness takes over, this battle stops and the body is allowed to heal. Diabetes is a very easy disease for healing.

"Lupus is another disease where we see constant healing. Fibromyalgia is similar. People with autoimmune diseases tend to have one thing in common—a deep-seated sense of unworthiness. Typically they were never nurtured, and developed a belief that they were not worthy of being cared for. Self-forgiveness is like water in a parched land for these people, and our ministry has seen every kind of autoimmune disease healed, although not always every person."

## Barbara Was Perfectly Ill

"Barbara is a good example of this. She was very ill with Chronic Fatigue Syndrome and multiple chemical sensitivities. Inwardly, Barbara felt that she had to be perfect, and had to be 100 percent right in all situations. Her adrenal glands had been constantly putting out too much adrenalin and cortisol from all this pressure and eventually had become exhausted.

"As Barbara began to understand the role that her thoughts and attitudes had played in her illness, she repented of looking to man for answers, and for the pressure she had placed upon herself to be perfect. She learned to trust God and believe that He always has our best interest at heart. She learned to accept His love and repented for believing the devil's lies. As she made these internal changes, her soul began to prosper, and she regained her good health."

## Satan's Lies Can Be Deadly

"There are many forms of bitterness that all come from the same source. That source is the original liar, satan. Satan started accusing God to human beings in Genesis 2 and continues to promote anxiety, anger, fear, and separation from God any way he can.

"Not only does he continually try to make us believe lies about ourselves, he lies about who God is, promoting the belief that God is an evil dictator, indifferent to our plight, and will punish us harshly for every mistake. We often unknowingly pass these beliefs on to our children, causing *the sin of the fathers* [to be passed on] *to the third and fourth generation* (Exod. 34:7 NIV).

"In reality, God is a loving Father, wholly good, who always has our best interest at heart. When we heal from the lies that satan has told us about our Father, ourselves, and others, we inherit a basic sense of trust and security. We become true sons and daughters of the Kingdom, able to do the works that Jesus did."

## Forgive or Forget?

There is a misconception that forgetting about a problem is the same as forgiving. Indeed, some painful memories are so well hidden we are not even aware of their effect on us. We may have forgotten, but if there is any pain in the memory, we have not forgiven.

Art illustrates how hidden pain can affect us. "An 80-year-old gentleman had suffered crippling migraines for 40 years. After we worked with him awhile, he became aware that his migraine headaches had started not long after his son had died in a car accident. He realized that he had blamed himself for that accident and had never been able to forgive himself.

"Self-blame is a very common characteristic of people who suffer migraines. What this man had done was to bury the painful memories and try to move on with his life. Even though he did not consciously think about it, those painful memories were affecting him deeply. When he chose to stop blaming himself, he was able to forgive himself. He gained peace with the memory and his migraine headaches were permanently stopped.

"The tendency to equate forgiveness with forgetting is what keeps many people from recognizing the roots of their illness. I myself had a difficult childhood and held a lot of hurt, but I had put it out of my mind and the memories rarely came to my thoughts. However, those buried memories were pockets of pain that continued to stress my immune system. They formed roots of bitterness that proved to be a big factor in the illness that nearly took my life. I had to dig out these forgotten memories and forgive them."

Forgetting puts a problem out of our minds, but it does not equal forgiveness. Forgetting removes the memory from our conscious mind but not from our deep memories.

## Biblical Forgiveness

The distinction between forgiving and forgetting is so important because *God's ability to forgive us is directly related to our willingness to forgive others.* Even the Lord's Prayer says, *'Forgive us our trespasses **as we forgive those who trespass against us**.'* Here are some other verses that describe this close relationship:

> *For if you forgive men their trespasses, your heavenly Father will also forgive you. But if you do not forgive men their trespasses, neither will your Father forgive your trespasses* (Matthew 6:14-15).

> *So My heavenly Father also will do to you, if each of you, from his heart, does not forgive his brother his trespasses* (Matthew 18:35).

> *And whenever you stand praying, if you have anything against anyone, forgive him, so that your Father in heaven may also forgive you your trespasses. But if you do not forgive, neither will your Father in heaven forgive your trespasses* (Mark 11:25-26).

*If we confess our sins he is faithful and just to forgive us our sins and to cleanse us from all unrighteousness* (1 John 1:9).

## The Power of Forgiveness

"Pain in a memory tells us that bitterness and unforgiveness are present. When we forgive, we make a choice to cancel the debt. This is part of enabling the pain in the memory to go away. As long as there is pain in a memory, forgiveness is not complete.

"When we forgive, we separate the person from what they did to us. We can forgive the person for having been used by the devil to cause harm. We do not forgive the sin; we forgive the person, just as Jesus did on the cross. He prayed, *'Father, forgive them, for they do not know what they do'* (Luke 23:34). When we forgive, we may still recall the event, but it has a different meaning to us. We have peace about it.

"We must forgive even if the other person deserves punishment. We must forgive even if the other person is not sorry for what they did. We are not excusing the person or saying we weren't hurt, we are saying, 'I am not your judge. I choose to cancel your debt to me.'

BIBLICAL FORGIVENESS IS SOMETHING WE
DO FOR OURSELVES AS AN ACT OF
OBEDIENCE AND HEALING.

"Biblical forgiveness is something we do for ourselves, as an act of obedience and healing. If we follow satan's plan, we may blame, or even hate, the offender. However, we will suffer the consequences of mental and physical distress in our own lives. If we follow God's plan, we will forgive, and release the burden. The result will be our own experience of healing, joy, peace, and even compassion for the other person."

## Learn to Dwell in Love!

"A blanket prayer of forgiveness does not work because every painful memory is a separate root of bitterness. Biblical forgiveness requires that we dig out every painful memory and deal with it specifically. To release healing, we have to work with the Holy Spirit to uncover painful memories and forgive the offenses, both the hurt and resentment we hold toward another person and the bitterness we may hold toward ourselves.

"In my own situation, I could feel myself getting better and better with each act of forgiveness, so that I got to the point where I would actually get excited and happy when I discovered a new bitter memory to forgive, because it meant even more freedom for me.

"Being offended is the absence of forgiveness and it is always sin. The Bible says, *He who dwells in love dwells in God* (see 1 John 4:16). The truth is that we cannot afford to hate our brother. For our own sake we must not let the sun go down on our anger (see Eph. 4:26). We do not have to remain offended or hurt. God has always made a way of escape. Too often we are taught that we don't have to obey this, and it is a missing link.

"There is always a blessing in obedience. When we count the high cost of unforgiveness to us, it is easy to see that we need to forgive for our own benefit. We know we have succeeded when we forgive to such an extent that compassion and prayer for the person who offended us take over."

## Renew Your Mind!

"Offenses and troubles are inevitable. And when we are hurt, the temptation is to blame the offender or God, leading to anger and resentment. Satan tempts us to do this—to blame others and stay in a basic state of stress and bitterness whether we are consciously aware of it or not. However, conscious or not, inner tension causes our bodies to be in a stressful state to some degree.

"Hebrews 4:12 says that the Word of God divides soul and spirit, *'For the word of God is quick and powerful, and sharper than any two-edged sword, piercing even to the dividing asunder of soul and spirit, and of the joints and marrow, and is a discerner of the thoughts and intents of the heart.'*

"Through bitterness, we come to live in a toxic thought process that we think is normal. We do not recognize our sin unless we compare how we really think and feel with the Word of God.

"Diseases cannot be separated from our thought processes. Every thought affects us. Good thoughts bring health to our bones and negative thoughts bring disease to our bones. Negative thoughts have a profound effect on our immune systems.

"Romans 12:2 says that you are *'transformed by the renewing of your mind.'* Hebrews 9:14 says that the blood of Jesus purges our conscience of all dead works or sin. As we conform to the Word of God and how He wants us to look at situations, our whole way of thinking changes. Our internal chemistry also changes. I believe we gain new neural pathways and new influences on genetic expression. We are transformed, living up to the promise to become a new creation in Messiah.

> *And do not be conformed to this world, but be transformed by the renewing of your mind, that you may prove what is that good and acceptable and perfect will of God* (Romans 12:2).

"We must put a stop to our stressful thought process in order to allow physical and emotional healing to progress. Although we may want to blame someone else, the key is to take responsibility for our own thoughts, feelings, and actions through biblical forgiveness.

"I really want to emphasize that point—*we are not responsible for having experienced the offense, but we are responsible for how we react to it.* If we follow satan's plan, we will blame, even hate, the offender, but if we do, we will suffer the consequences of mental and physical distress in our own lives. If we follow God's plan, we will forgive and release the burden."

## What About Repeating Patterns?

Art believes that forgiveness is important even in situations in which the other person is predictably going to do the same offense to us again and again. An example might be a boss or family member who is a critical or difficult person. In those cases, we can forgive right now for what we know they will do tomorrow. Forgiveness in a present situation can prevent pain from forming.

Forgiveness is not the same as approving of their behavior, and it does not mean accepting abuse or mistreatment. It means that even as you take care of yourself and do what is right, you do not sit in judgment on the offender.

## Forgiving Satanic Ritual Abuse

A woman came to Art for ministry after a lifetime of abuse by her parents, who were satan worshipers. He says, "This lady was very sick with a number of serious health conditions. Her parents had been satanists and had subjected her to horrific satanic ritual abuse. When people have been abused or sexually assaulted, they usually feel angry, unclean, and violated. They also tend to feel ashamed and to blame themselves. This lady had all of these feelings and a number of very serious health conditions.

"To overcome this, she had to go through all the specific memories of the abuse she had suffered, forgiving and seeking the Lord's truth for each situation. By rooting out each bitter memory, she was able to forgive her parents and others connected with the abuse. As she did so, she experienced complete healing and an infusion of joy.

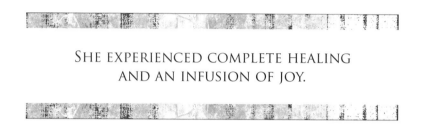

SHE EXPERIENCED COMPLETE HEALING
AND AN INFUSION OF JOY.

"What she had experienced was terrible, but the real agent of her suffering was the devil. The devil had deceived her parents and motivated all the horrible acts that she suffered. This understanding enabled her to forgive her parents for what they had done to her, but she would never again put herself in a situation where such acts could be repeated.

> *The thief does not come except to steal, and to kill, and to destroy. I have come that they may have life, and that they may have it more abundantly* (John 10:10).

> *For this purpose the Son of God was manifested, that He might destroy the works of the devil* (1 John 3:8).

## Forgiveness Destroys the Devil's Works

"To forgive does not mean to excuse what the other party did. It does not justify what was done to you. It simply means you are not going to be their judge or be the one to hold them to account. It means that you deliberately separate the sin from the sinner.

"You can be angry about the sin, but have compassion and forgiveness for the sinner. Even at the cross, Jesus prayed for those who were driving nails into His hands.

"If we stay in anger, satan can control us. That is why Ephesians 4 says, *'Do not let the sun go down on your wrath [anger].'* We will still recall the event, but anger toward the perpetrator is gone. *There is no shame or guilt, and the Holy Spirit restores everything that the devil tried to steal.*

"A profound change occurs when we recognize that what the person did was wrong, but that the act and the person are separate. We do not forgive the action, which was a sin. We forgive the person who hurt or offended us. This releases satan's control.

"The devil wants to attack and destroy your health, your family, your peace, and even your life. He is the real enemy that we must combat, not the person who was the vehicle of his action. However, nothing happens until we do what the Bible says. We can know everything about the Bible and Jesus' teachings, but if we don't do it, it does no good.

## The Effects of the Sins of the Father

"Resentment, fears, shame, worry, or any other form of sin in our lives gives the devil a place from which he can attack (see Eph. 4:27). He can even attack children through their parents.

"When I was ministering at a conference in India, a pastor's wife told me about her 5-year-old son who had severe asthma. He was 300 miles away at their home. He was healed when she repented for not trusting God for the provision to take care of her children. She told me that when she had become pregnant, she and her husband were struggling financially and very fearful—they believed they could not afford another child. After I led her in prayer, she then blessed the child and he was immediately healed and is still healed today."

# Closing Thoughts

Painful memories may be forgotten, but they do not stop affecting our health. They continue to exert a poison deep inside us that the Bible calls a root of bitterness.

To be fully healed physically or emotionally, it is necessary to dig out each painful memory and repent, forgive, or receive forgiveness.

We do not forget or excuse the offense, we forgive the person; and the Holy Spirit changes our understanding of the situation so that there is no more pain. We can measure forgiveness because with complete forgiveness, the pain is gone, but the memory remains. We can relate to the memory in a different way because it does not hurt.

When we recall the event, there is no physiological reaction; our mind is renewed, and our conscience is purged. The joy of the Lord comes in; compassion and peace replace anger, fear, anxiety, resentment, shame, and bitterness.

Art concludes, "Hosea says that even God's people are destroyed for lack of knowledge. That is what motivates my heart for ministry. I see the devil destroying lives with his lies. I see otherwise good people perishing because they do not have the knowledge to combat these lies.

"That is why I wrote the book, *Biblical Foundations of Freedom*. God wants everyone to be free, healthy, and prosperous, but there are certain things that we must do to obtain this."

# What You Can Do

There are four steps in working through memories:

**Step 1—Forgive or Repent.** In obedience we choose to forgive or repent. (See Matthew 6:14-15; James 4:7; 1 John 1:9.)

**Step 2—Cancel Satan's Authority.** In the name of Jesus and by the power of His blood, we cancel satan's authority over us in the issue. (See Ephesians 4:27; James 4:7.)

**Step 3—Ask the Holy Spirit for Healing.** Ask to be healed of a broken heart or a broken body, free from shame, anger, guilt, rejection, bitterness, or fear. We seek the renewing of our minds, or the purging of our consciences. (See Psalm 103:3; Romans 12:1-2; Luke 4:18-19; Hebrews 9:14.)

**Step 4—Listen for God's Truth About the Situation.** Ask the Holy Spirit to tell you His truth about this situation. The Holy Spirit talks to us in a quiet voice, dreams, visions, impressions, or just takes the pain and leaves His peace. (See John 14:26.)

# The Forgiveness Prayer

"Heavenly Father, I purpose and choose to forgive _____ (the person) for what was done. I release him/her and cancel their debt to me completely. In the name of Jesus and through the power of His blood, I cancel all of satan's authority over me in this memory because it is forgiven. Holy Spirit, heal my heart and tell me Your truth about this situation." Listen to what the Lord says to you.

# The Repentance Prayer

"Heavenly Father, forgive me for _____ (the specific act). I purpose and choose to forgive myself. In the name of Jesus and through the power of His blood, I cancel all of satan's authority over me in this sin. I am forgiven. Holy Spirit, heal my heart and tell me Your truth about this situation." Listen to what the Lord says to you.

\* \* \*

# Endnote

1. Art's book, *Biblical Foundations of Freedom,* provides the foundations for basic discipleship in this area, and we encourage everyone to read it. All proceeds from the book go to supporting the outreach work of his ministry. For more information about Dr. Art Mathias and his ministry, visit his Wellspring Ministries Website at www.akwellspring.com.

# Chapter 6

# Healed With the Father's Blessing
## *Craig Hill*

*When Esau heard the words of his father, he cried with
an exceedingly great and bitter cry, and said to his father,
Bless me—me also, O my father!* (Genesis 27:34)

Craig Hill has discovered that the father's blessing is one of the most powerful determinants of success in life. He has found that no matter what the person's age, the need to feel this blessing is very strong. The cry of Esau to Jacob reflects the cry of all human hearts. Craig explains how we can use this insight to find healing.

"This cry from the heart of the son, Esau, to his father, Isaac, is the cry of many adult or adolescent children toward their own fathers and mothers. It is evident that God intended for every child to be blessed by his or her father and mother at many times in life. Throughout the entire Bible, we see Hebrew parents laying hands on their children and imparting a blessing with words and actions. In the biblical account of the blessing that Isaac was to impart to his sons, we see the power and importance of this blessing."

# The Importance of the Father's Blessing

"Isaac and his wife and sons all understood that the blessing of a father upon his firstborn son had tremendous power to cause that son and his family to prosper for generations into the future. This blessing was understood to be so powerful that Jacob, with the help of his mother, Rebecca, was willing to lie, cheat, and deceive in order to obtain the blessing of his father that rightfully should have belonged to his brother, Esau.

"As we read in Genesis 27, Jacob, pretending to be his brother, Esau, was able to convince his partially-blind father that he was indeed Esau, and thereby received from his father the blessing of the firstborn. When Esau subsequently came to his father to receive his blessing and discovered that his brother, Jacob, had already received from their father an irrevocable blessing, Scripture records the following:

> And Esau said to his father, "Have you only one blessing, my father? Bless me—me also, O my father!" And Esau lifted up his voice and wept (Genesis 27:38).

> So Esau hated Jacob because of the blessing with which his father blessed him, and Esau said in his heart, "The days of mourning for my father are at hand; then I will kill my brother Jacob" (Genesis 27:41).

# The Father Holds the Key

"Why was Esau so angry and hurt over the paternal blessing being given to his brother instead of to him? He was devastated because he understood something that very few people understand in our modern times. Esau knew that a father holds in his hand a key to the future prosperity of his children. When a father uses the key of blessing in the lives of his children, he releases them to prosper.

"When we follow the life of Jacob through several generations, we observe that Jacob and his family multiplied in number, became exceedingly wealthy, remained healthy and did not experience plagues and sickness, and conquered their enemies and ruled in their land for many generations. Esau, on the other hand, did not prosper, and his family did not become large in number, did not become wealthy, and was frequently conquered by enemies."

## Children Blessed by Parents Tend to Prosper

I have observed this same phenomenon in many modern-day families. Children who are blessed by their parents tend to prosper in their adult lives, and children who were never blessed by their parents tend to languish and not prosper. Why is this? I believe it is because blessing is a custom established by God and meant to function in every family on earth. Blessing is God's primary mechanism of imparting His image (thoughts, feelings, and experience) of **identity** *(Who am I?)* and **destiny** *(Why am I here?)* deep into the heart of a person. This is of critical importance because vision for life, physical and emotional health, financial prosperity, and family relational dynamics are all directly linked to images of God, self, and others imprinted in the inner man (heart) of every person. *'As he thinks in his heart, so is he'* (Prov. 23:7).

"We have seen many people experience supernatural physical and emotional healing the moment they allowed God to remove a deep-seated false image in their hearts and replace it with an impartation from God of His truth. In most such cases, the inner false image had come during childhood through the lack of blessing from parents or even the opposite, direct cursing by parents."

## Whose Image Is in Your Heart?

"So what is blessing and its opposite, cursing? I would define these words this way: Blessing is God's mechanism of impartation of His image of identity and destiny to the hearts of people. Cursing is satan's mechanism of impartation of his image of identity and destiny to the hearts of people. In Hebrew, the word to bless is the word *baruch*. The literal meaning of this word is 'to kneel before someone.'

"However, the primary spiritual connotation is *to empower to prosper*. So when you bless someone, you kneel before them in humility and literally empower that person to prosper. I don't believe that this word, prosper, is only applied to finances. If you bless your son, you empower him to prosper in every area of his life—his spiritual life with God, his physical health, his emotional well-being, his marriage, his children, his finances, his career, and his ministry.

"To curse is to do the opposite. If you curse your son, you likewise cripple, disable, or disempower him from prospering in all of these same areas of life. In the Greek, the word to bless is the word *eulogia*. The literal meaning of this word is "to speak well of." Perhaps you have already picked up on the English word, eulogy, which comes from this same root. A eulogy, of course, also has the meaning 'to speak well of someone,' but unfortunately is usually spoken at a funeral. Obviously, that which is spoken at a funeral will not empower the dead person to prosper. In order to empower one to prosper, a blessing must be spoken while the person is yet living and can receive the blessing. So to curse is to speak evil of someone, or to speak satan's vision or image into someone's life; while to bless is to impart God's vision and image into a person's life."

## The Jewish Tradition of Blessing the Family

"God has given the Jewish people a wonderful tradition of weekly family blessing that is still practiced to this day by many families. I am speaking of the tradition of gathering the family once a week on Erev Shabbat (Friday evening) for a special meal together and a pronouncement of blessing. (With the busy schedule of most families, for many this would be a miracle in and of itself just to be able to have a meal together once a week.) Each week at this time, the Jewish father prays a blessing over his wife. He then pronounces a Hebrew blessing over each of his children.

"In many Jewish families, the father also proclaims vision and prosperity over his children, thus creating an expectation in the children of future success and prosperity. By so doing, such a father, whether he knows it or not, is imparting God's image into the hearts and minds of his children. In many Jewish families in which this is practiced, the words of blessing that the father is speaking over his children are prophetic, and the children fulfill in adult life exactly what their father prophesied weekly."

## Words Affect Children's Future

"I have also observed that in some Christian families, the primary words children hear from their parents are words of correction and criticism. Sometimes the words that parents speak actually impart satan's vision and image rather than God's. Most parents are blind to the power that their words and actions have to bless or curse the lives of their children. For example, a father may say to his 15-year-old daughter, 'You're not going out of the house in those clothes. Why, you look like a prostitute! If you keep dressing like that and hanging around with your current friends, you'll probably be pregnant within a year.' Such words from parents are also prophetic and have the potential for children to fulfill exactly what their parents have prophesied. In many such Christian families there are only words of correction and no regular weekly time of blessing, as there is in some Jewish homes.

MOST PARENTS ARE BLIND TO THE POWER THAT
THEIR WORDS AND ACTIONS HAVE TO BLESS OR
CURSE THE LIVES OF THEIR CHILDREN.

"As I studied this topic of blessing and cursing in the Bible, I identified six critical times in a child's life in which blessing was meant to be received from God through parents, and a seventh time at which children were meant to bless their parents. The following is a brief list of the seven times: 1. Conception, 2. During time in the womb, 3. Birth, 4. Infancy, 5. Puberty (rite of passage), 6. Marriage, and 7. During old age. Growing up in the ancient Hebrew culture, it would have been almost impossible to miss out on being blessed at all seven of these critical times. The culture was structured so that both ceremonial and day-to-day blessing naturally happened in most families. This resulted in spiritual, emotional, physical, relational, and financial health for such families who practiced blessing.

"Unfortunately for most modern-day families, such customs and traditions originally placed by God in our culture have systematically been eliminated. As a result, most parents today would not even know when the seven critical times of blessing are, let alone how to bless their children at any of these times. Furthermore, since most of our own parents also did not have the knowledge or experience of blessing while growing up, they were neither able to provide us the experience of blessing at these seven critical times, nor raise us in a culture and lifestyle of blessing.

"As a consequence, it is very difficult for those of us who are now parents to give to our children something—blessing—we have never received ourselves. Many adult children are left with the same deep inner heart cry of Esau, '*Bless me—me also, O my father.*'"

## Receiving the Blessing

"At this point, you may be asking, 'What can I do now to personally receive the missed blessing, and how can I bless my children? How can I establish a culture of blessing in my family and now initiate a cycle of blessing for all future generations?'"

"As a result of so many people asking exactly these questions, in 1988 God led my wife, Jan, and me to begin a ministry that is designed to provide people with not only the knowledge, but also primarily with the heart experience of receiving blessing missed from parents, directly from God. Through this ministry, Family Foundations International (FFI), we have trained thousands of teams in over 40 countries around the world to lead people through a spiritual process resulting in a supernatural experience of blessing with the Father. For many people, this is a life-changing experience, as deep-rooted false images and experiential lies are removed by the power of God and replaced deep within the heart by truth.

"I believe that the best way to initiate and establish a culture of blessing in your own family now would be to personally attend one of our seminars. However, even before doing this, I've listed three simple things that you can immediately implement in your family:

1. Consider establishing a weekly practice of gathering your family for a meal together on Erev Shabbat, Friday evening. Before coming together, as parents ask God if there are any ways in which you have sinned against or wounded your children over the past week. Then at the table, before the meal, confess anything that God has shown you to each child, repent, and ask forgiveness from that child. Make sure to make eye contact while doing so. After repentance, then spend a few minutes praying for and speaking a personal blessing over each of your children.

2. Consider making a practice of praying blessing over each other as husband and wife daily. This is not a 'prayer meeting.' I am talking about six minutes a day. I suggest the following way to pray for each other. Find a consistent time that works for you as a couple. Face each other and pray with your eyes open, looking into each other's eyes. (Plan to convey blessing not only with words, but also with your eyes.) Spend one minute each in prayer on each of the following three topics: A. Repent of and ask forgiveness for anything God shows you regarding how you have

wounded or sinned against your spouse in the past 24 hours; B. Pray a prayer thanking God for your wife or husband and for qualities you appreciate about her or him; C. Pronounce blessing over your spouse and her or his day.

3. Consider planning and conducting a rite of passage blessing ceremony for any of your sons or daughters who have reached or passed the age of puberty.[1]"

## The Connection Between Blessing and Health

"Over the years, we have found that there is a very strong connection between blessing and physical and emotional health. Lack of blessing, or sometimes cursing, is frequently correlated with physical sickness and lack of emotional, relational, and financial well-being. We have observed that when people have received an impartation of blessing from God the Father, many times they have immediately experienced physical and emotional healing. I believe the reason for this is found in Third John 1:2, *'Beloved, I pray that you may prosper in all things and be in health, just as your soul prospers.'*

"Blessing means to empower to prosper, and is God's mechanism of imparting His image and vision into the soul of a person. So blessing causes the soul of a person to prosper, which according to the Bible results in health and prosperity in all areas of life."

## Supernatural Healing Through the Father's Blessing

"The following are just a few of the stories relating to supernatural physical, emotional, and relational healing we have seen occur through receiving blessing from God the Father in one of our seminars and through the blessing of an earthly father and mother. In many of these cases, healing has come after a person has repented of bitterness toward and forgiven a parent who had cursed him or her and then received the blessing of God the Father. Whether or not you are able to attend one of our seminars, my prayer is that you will receive a supernatural understanding of the power of the blessing and will begin to enjoy similar fruit in your own life.

"We received the following accounts from William and Ruby Su, the leaders of our ministry team in the Philippines.

"A young woman in her early twenties who attended one of our seminars had suffered for many years with endometriosis, cysts in her ovaries, and had not had any menstrual periods for over three years. When she forgave her father who had abused her in childhood, she received a powerful blessing from her heavenly Father. She found that her female reproductive organs had returned to normal. She began experiencing normal menstrual cycles, and after an exam and ultrasound, her OB/GYN doctor could no longer find any evidence of any ovarian cysts or symptoms of endometriosis.

AFTER FORGIVING HER FATHER AND
RECEIVING THE FATHER'S BLESSING, SHE
WAS RELEASED FROM SEVERE BACK PAIN.

"On another island, a 52-year-old woman came who, as a child, had been unjustly beaten by a very stern father, and many times blamed for things that she had not done. Now her elderly father had just come to live with her and her family. After forgiving her father and receiving the Father's blessing, she was released from severe back pain with which she had suffered for many years. Others in the group noticed that a significant curve in the base of her neck was instantly healed and became straight."

# Stroke Symptoms Completely Healed

"A young woman shared that all of her adult life she had struggled with an overwhelming feeling of hatred toward her father who had rejected, cursed, and abandoned her as a little girl. She shared that this feeling of hatred was so strong that even after her father's death she could not forgive him. This young woman had also recently suffered a stroke and her legs were paralyzed and twisted.

"After forgiving her father and receiving a revelation of and blessing from God as her Father, this woman reported that all the feelings of hatred and bitterness were supernaturally gone and that she would now like to forgive and honor the memory of her earthly father. As she did so, others in the group were amazed as her legs instantly became straight, returned to normal, and she was healed of all remaining symptoms of the stroke. They reported that she immediately shouted for joy and glorified the name of God."

# Infertility Healed

"I have found that in families, not only is the blessing of the father important, but the words and blessing, or lack thereof, from the mother is also very impacting in the life of her children. God also intended every child to receive His image and impartation from both a father and a mother.

"Emily had been married for 13 years and had dreamed all her life of becoming a mother. Shortly after her wedding, Emily found that she was infertile, and over the course of the next 13 years tried without success every known type of medical treatment to become pregnant.

"Emily asked the Lord to reveal to her anything that might be connected with her infertility. Within seconds she was reliving several experiences in childhood in which her mother had imparted satan's lie and image to her heart by saying emphatically, 'You will never be a mother.' This lie had deeply taken root in Emily's heart and her body had apparently cooperated to fulfill this prophetic curse from the mother.

"After forgiving her mother, and allowing the Lord to replace the lie in her heart with His truth regarding her identity as a mother, Emily felt much lighter than when she had come to the seminar. Fifteen days later, Emily reported that she was now pregnant and expecting her first child. God had physically healed her female organs when she forgave her mother for cursing her and received God's blessing and truth in the depths of her heart. At the time of this writing, Emily has given birth to two beautiful, healthy children and is a wonderful, loving mother."

## The Father's Blessing Heals a Marriage

"Pablo was deeply saddened as he received the news from his father that his mother, who had been separated from his father for nine months, was not willing to return to the marriage and was now seeking a divorce. As Pablo pondered what he might do or pray to help his parents, a very strange thought came to him. He had recently observed a powerful change in the life of his 21-year-old son, who had been quite directionless and indecisive. This son could not decide if he wanted to enroll in Bible school, the university, or get a job. Consequently, he was sitting at home doing nothing. Pablo told me that when he looked into the eyes of his son, he saw a scared little boy who didn't know what to do and was afraid to make a decision.

"About that time, Pablo and his wife attended one of our seminars and realized that the probable reason that their son was directionless was that he had never been blessed by his father, and consequently was still spiritually and emotionally tied to his mother as a little boy. These parents then arranged a blessing ceremony for their son, which turned out to be life-changing for him. Pablo told me that immediately after the ceremony, when he looked into his son's eyes, for the first time, he saw looking back at him a confident, 21-year-old man, not a scared little boy. The spiritual and emotional umbilical cord had been cut with his mother. Shortly after, Pablo's son enrolled in the university and began to pursue a course of study toward a career into which he was certain God had called him.

"Upon receiving news of his parents' impending divorce, the strange thought that now came to Pablo was the remembrance of recently looking into his 64-year-old father's eyes and seeing the same "scared little boy look" that he had seen in his son before he had conducted the blessing ceremony for him. He now realized that his father, Luis, had never been blessed by his father and was still, at age 64, emotionally tied as a little boy to his mother. The reason that Luis had struggled in his relationship with his wife all of their married life was that he had never emotionally left his father and mother so he could properly cleave to his wife. *Therefore shall a man leave his father and his mother and shall cleave unto his wife: and they shall be one flesh'* (Gen. 2:24 KJV).

HE REALIZED THAT HIS FATHER HAD NEVER
BEEN BLESSED BY HIS FATHER AND WAS
STILL EMOTIONALLY TIED AS A LITTLE BOY
TO HIS MOTHER.

"Armed with this understanding, Pablo placed a telephone call to his 87-year-old grandfather, who was living in the country of their family's origin. Grandpa was quite shocked as Pablo tried to explain to him his request to come impart his blessing to his son, Luis, and release him to be a man in a Bar Barakah (Christian Bar Mitzvah) ceremony to be held on Luis's 65th birthday. Grandpa exclaimed, 'You want me to do what? My son is having his 65th birthday celebration. If he is not a man yet, he never will be.' However, Pablo was insistent and Grandpa finally agreed to come.

"Upon arrival, Pablo was able to explain to his grandfather the key of blessing that he held in his hand as a father, and that Luis was still emotionally bound to his mother as a little boy, with the cry of Esau, *'Bless me—me also, O my father,'* still in his heart at age 65. Grandpa still didn't entirely understand, but did agree that he would attempt to pray over and bless his son, Luis, on his 65th birthday.

"When the day of the ceremony arrived, after a time of worship to God, Grandpa and Luis sat opposite each other in two chairs. Grandpa first attempted to tell his son, 'I love you,' but only got out the first couple of syllables and broke into tears. Luis immediately broke into tears as well, and all either man could do for the next ten minutes was sit and weep. When Grandpa tried again to tell his son he loved him, they both broke into tears again. Finally the third time, Grandpa was able to tell his son he loved him and how proud he was of him. He told Luis that he was a huge success because all three of Luis's children loved the Lord, had married godly spouses, and all of Luis's grandchildren were born again and serving Yeshua. 'What greater legacy could a man ever ask for than that?'

"Then Grandpa asked, 'Son, do you remember when you were 15 years old?' As his father asked this question, Luis's eyes squinted as a huge surge of emotional pain began to be released. Yes, Luis remembered when he was 15 years old. What no one else knew was that at that time, Luis and his father had engaged in a huge argument that even became physical. Luis's father had become enraged at him that day, and had screamed at him horrible things, told him that he was worthless, and physically threw him out of the house. He told him he hated him and hoped he would never see this worthless son again.

"Luis, of course, had become equally angry, had said horrible things to his father and also told him he hated him and never would see him again. He left the house in rebellion at age 15 to begin his adult life.

Obviously, this was not the blessing his heart was looking for to release him into his adult identity. Since that time, Luis and his father had reconciled their relationship, but had never spoken of this event. As his father now brought it up 50 years later, it immediately stirred to the surface 50 years of bitterness, hatred, resentment, and anger that had been in Luis's heart since that day.

"Years ago, he had voiced the words, 'I forgive my father,' but his heart had never released the pain, and he had neither truly forgiven his father from his heart nor repented of the bitterness, dishonor, or rebellion that had been in his heart toward his father.

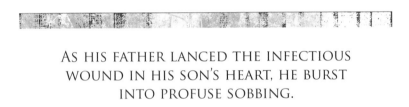

## AS HIS FATHER LANCED THE INFECTIOUS WOUND IN HIS SON'S HEART, HE BURST INTO PROFUSE SOBBING.

"Now 50 years later, as his father lanced the infectious wound in his son's heart, a deep, anguished cry escaped from the heart of his son as he burst into profuse sobbing. Luis fell forward and buried his face in his father's chest, his father also sobbing profusely. When Grandpa's sobs had subsided enough to speak, he whispered to Luis, 'Son, I'm so sorry. I was wrong that day. Please forgive me. I got angry, said things I didn't mean, and cursed you rather than blessing you. Please forgive me. I love you!' These words only intensified the sobbing of the son.

"When Luis's sobbing finally subsided, he sat up and looked his father in the eyes. His father returned the gaze, then asked him directly, 'Son, I love you. I was wrong. Will you forgive me for the words I said and the way I treated you growing up in general, and specifically on that day when you left home?' Luis responded, 'Yes Papa, I forgive you. I love you. I also was wrong in my attitude of dishonor and rebellion and the words I spoke.

Will you forgive me?' Grandpa responded, 'Yes, of course. I love you, son. And today, I pronounce over you the words I should have spoken fifty years ago. Son, I'm proud of you. You are not a foolish little boy. You are a man. Today I bless you. I cut you loose emotionally and spiritually from your mother, and I give you my blessing and release you into your adult identity as a man. Go and be and do all God has called you to.'

"Pablo said that something supernatural had happened in the heart of his father, Luis, through the blessing of his father. Pablo told me that later that day, when he looked into his father's eyes, for the first time in his life, he saw a bold, confident 65-year-old man who was at peace inside, rather than the scared, angry little boy.

"The supernatural healing that took place that day in Luis's heart was so profound that two weeks later his wife, Pablo's mother, cancelled the divorce and moved back home. She said, 'I don't know what happened to my husband, but finally I got back the man I thought I married forty-five years ago. For the last forty-five years I have been trying to follow an angry little boy, who didn't know where he was going, and who was frequently blaming me for many of his own failures and frustrations. Somehow, now the fear, anger, frustration, and blame are all gone. This is the man I fell in love with forty-five years ago. I don't want to divorce him. I love him and want to live the rest of my life with him.'

"Luis and his wife spent the next several months living in a honeymoon. They spent many more years prospering in business and devoting much of their time to ministering to and helping other couples through a marriage ministry in their city. Luis later told Pablo, 'I had no idea that the blessing of my father was what my heart had been longing for, for over fifty years. I knew it would be good to see my father, but I had no idea that his blessing would be such a key to change my image and experience of myself and of life.'

"Grandpa later told Pablo, 'If I had known that my blessing as a father was the key that would unlock future prosperity to my son, I would have used it many decades ago. I only regret that I made this discovery so late in my son's life, and that it took my grandson to motivate me to do what I should have done as a father many decades ago.'"

\* \* \*

To find a Blessing Generations, Ancient Paths Experience seminar near you, please visit Craig Hill's Website at www.familyfoundations.com. For more information on how you can host an Ancient Paths Experience in your local congregation, please contact info@familyfoundations.com.

## Endnote

1. For more information on how to practically implement the three suggestions, see the Family Foundations International Website: www.familyfoundations.com/blessing.

Chapter 7

# God's Justice System
## *Pastor Don Dickerman*

*In My name they shall cast out demons* (Mark 16:17).

Almost everyone wonders about demons—if they are real, what they can do to people, and how they operate. Don Dickerman has become an expert on this topic. In the past 20 years, Don has ministered in more than 850 prisons and has helped free more than 25,000 men and women from demonic powers. He has learned how demons can cause disease and other problems, and how to get them to leave.

One of the most important things he has learned is that God has a justice system. Demons cannot oppress us unless they gain a legal consent to do so. They gain that consent through unforgiveness, unrepented sin, involvement with the occult, drug and alcohol addiction, and through a variety of other means.

Demons have no right to oppress someone who has truly repented, and that truth can be used to force them to leave. Don says, "When confronted with the truth, demons have to leave. I consider myself part of God's justice system. I am the believer's defense attorney. I have learned that the truth will always set you free."

# Prison Ministry Was Discouraging

Don came to his understanding of demons through his work with prisoners. In the early years of his ministry, Don preached the love of God in many prisons. He saw that the inmates often developed a genuine faith, but something drew them back to their old ways once they were out of prison.

While in prison, they would go to Bible studies, read their Bibles and pray, but when they got out, it would only take five or six months before most of them fell back into their crime patterns and were returned to prison.

After years of seeing so much recidivism, Don was losing heart. He said, "I prayed about it constantly, asking God what I was missing that so many just went back to their old ways.

"I was feeling particularly low when I was ministering in a Galveston, Texas, prison. I had come back to my motel, and I felt so frustrated that I lay on my bed and wept. I asked God, 'Why can't I get people out of bondage? What am I missing? I want to be a deliverer!' I did not imagine what a profound change in my life was ahead of me after this prayer."

# A Prophetic Vision Revealed the Answer

"Not long after this prayer, I went to preach in a federal prison in Three Rivers, Texas, near San Antonio. A corrections officer was in the audience listening to my sermon. We left the service together and as we walked to our cars, he told me that he was studying for the ministry and wanted to be a counselor in the prison system.

"We both left the prison at the same time and were heading in the same direction, toward Corpus Christi. When I stopped at a gas station, he pulled in behind me and came over to my window, seeming excited about something.

"He told me about a vision that he had while I was preaching back at the prison. In the vision, I was standing in a pot of bubbling oil surrounded by sick people. The oil began to bubble up and run down my arms. As it touched the people they were healed. Then he said, 'Get ready brother. God is fixin' to pour it out on you.'"

## Strange Things Started Happening

Don knew this vision was from the Holy Spirit, but he did not know what to make of it. He had come from a Baptist background where dreams and visions are not often mentioned. He certainly had never seen supernatural healing and deliverance, and was completely unprepared to see this in his own services.

He describes what started to occur: "I continued to preach at the prisons just as I had before, but there was now a difference—people were getting healed right there in the service! I started to get letters from the men saying things like, 'While you were preaching, heat came over me and I was healed.'

"I gave altar calls for the inmates and sometimes people fell down under the power of the Holy Spirit without my even touching them. I had never seen this sort of thing before. I was amazed at the healing and spiritual manifestations; I knew it was God at work, and I had deep gratitude to Him, but no understanding.

"As these healings continued to happen, my boldness increased and I began to expect it. I was overwhelmed, and sometimes after the services I would weep from joy and gratitude. It was very humbling."

## Visions About Healing

"I started having visions related to healing—not often—but always accurate. The first healing was through a vision at one of the prisons in Huntsville, Texas. I was in the prison chapel with about 400 inmates. There was praise music being played and I was sitting, waiting for my time to speak.

"As I sat there, I saw a vision of a dark, ugly rat with jagged teeth inside someone's colon, gnawing away at it. I felt that someone would be healed, so I cautiously got up and spoke that somebody was going to be healed in his colon.

"Although I got up and said that, I had no idea really what was going to happen. I sensed it was the Holy Spirit giving me the Word about healing, but I thought there was a chance it was just my imagination.

"As soon as I spoke the words, an inmate jumped up and started saying 'That's me! That's me! That's me!' I prayed for him and he went back to his seat. But I knew that he was not the one.

"At the close of the service the others were filing back to their cell blocks. An inmate came up and put a note in my pocket. I pulled the note out and read it, and it said 'I'm the one.'

"He had just come back from the prison hospital in terrible pain with an abdominal swelling, like a big knot hanging over his belt. He told me he needed surgery, but since he was getting out soon, they were not going to treat it.

"This inmate pulled up his shirt and I saw a knot right above his belt buckle. I knew he was the one I was supposed to pray for. I laid my hands on that spot and commanded demon powers to leave him and for healing to come.

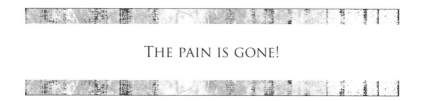

## THE PAIN IS GONE!

"He threw up blood and bile—it was an ugly situation, but some of the other inmates got towels and cleaned it up. I walked to the door and he went back to his cell saying, 'The pain is gone!'

"The next month when I was there again to preach, he met me at the door and said, 'Brother Don, I don't have any pain!' I was overwhelmed because I knew that I did not have anything to do with it. It was a confirmation of the Holy Spirit revealing something to me. The power of God had cast out a demon of illness."

## Confronting Demons

Don knew demons were real, but not much more than that. He began his deliverance ministry by a kind of divine accident. He says, "A female inmate at a women's prison in Ontario, Canada, had been writing to me and had told me she felt that she had demonic oppression and wanted me to help her.

"This woman, Kathy, had been raised in a home where she suffered satanic ritual abuse and knew what she was dealing with. I worked with her by mail over a period of months to repent of past actions and forgive those who had harmed her, as these are doorways for demons to come into a person's life.

"When she was ready, I contacted a minister who was experienced with deliverance and went through the lengthy process to get permission to do this deliverance at the prison. On the day appointed, I arrived at the prison, but I found that the other minister was not able to arrive as he had planned.

"However, Kathy was prepared, so I decided to try to do it myself. I told her that I would 'bind the demons.' When I said this, her facial expression completely changed. She got a strange look and a weird intensity came into her eyes. Kathy started talking in a man's voice. I knew the demons were present.

"Speaking in a man's voice, the demon said, 'I am going to kill you. Someone is going to die today and it is going to be you.' I said, 'I am washed in the blood of Jesus and the power of death and life is in my tongue, not yours.' Then I commanded the demon to apologize to me, and he did. We are *somebody* in Christ. It is exciting that a demon has to bow in the name of Jesus—every time.

"I began to bind the demons and commanded them to reveal their names because Jesus had done this with the demons of Gadara. As they gave their names, I bound them and commanded them to leave her. This was a very dramatic deliverance; usually it is not much more than prayer.

"Kathy was instantly changed. Her face looked younger, and she had a sense of joy and peace. She remains free of torment to this day."

## Scriptural Authority Concerning Demons

There is abundant scriptural teaching about demons, but very little is taught in the churches. Don has done extensive scriptural research.

- Many think that teaching about deliverance from demons has no place in modern Christianity. However, in Matthew 10:1-8, the disciples were told to heal the sick, cleanse the lepers, cast out demons, and raise the dead.

- When the seventy disciples (representative of Christians) were sent out with authority, they marveled that even the spirits were subject to them. (See Luke 10:1-9;17-19.)

- Believers were told to cast out devils in Jesus' name. (See Mark 16:17.)

- Evil spirits are often responsible for sickness and disease. (See Luke 8:2; 13:11.)

- The Bible says that Jesus went about doing good and healing all those who were oppressed by the devil. (See Acts 10:38.)

- In all there are over 100 references to devils, seducing spirits, and demons in the New Testament. It is clear that demonic powers exist and are arrayed in a hierarchy. (See Ephesians 6:12.)"

# Misconceptions

"The most common misconception is that only evil people can have demons. Nothing could be further from the truth. If you are alive, you are a candidate for satan's attack.

"Another misconception is that the Holy Spirit and demons cannot exist in the same person. That is what most people find troubling. Demons do take up residence in the body and in the soul, but they cannot take up residence in the spirit. The Holy Spirit abides in the spirit of the believer.

POSSESSION IS OWNERSHIP.

"Demons do not possess the body as characterized in Hollywood. Possession is ownership. Believers are 'owned' by the Holy Spirit. However, oppression can and does take place in the soul and in the flesh. Where do anger, hatred, and bitterness live? Where does lust manifest if not the body and soul?

"The soul—the mind, will, and emotions—is the area of torment, and that is where demons do their dirty deeds. This is the warfare that Paul talks about so often in the Scriptures. It is reclaiming our territory that constitutes the process of sanctification.

"That this process of fighting demonic oppression continues even after the new birth is exemplified in the following passages:

- Believers were given anointing for discerning of spirits. (See First John 2:20,27.)

- The Bible teaches believers to resist the devil and stand firm in their faith. (See First Peter 5:9.)

- The Bible teaches how to identify spirits that are not of God. (See First John 4:1-3.)

- The Bible talks about tearing down strongholds built in the mind by the enemy and that the believer's weapons are spiritual and mighty through God. (See Second Corinthians 10:3-5.)

- The Bible teaches that it is the shield of faith that resists the demons' fiery darts. (See Ephesians 6:16.)"

## God's Kingdom Has Rules

"The truth is that demons can attack anyone who opens a door to them, but demons must have that door opened. They must have a legal right to enter a person's life. Jesus says in Revelation 3:20, *'Behold I stand at the door and knock.'* Why does He knock at our door? It is because He must have our permission to enter our lives.

"Demons also must have permission, or entryways. They cannot intrude at will but must have legal consent from the person or from God. Consent is anything that opens a doorway to the demon."

## Demon Doorways

"Consent can be as simple as accepting the presence of a Ouija board or participating in other occult practices including trances, hypnosis, and séances. One of the most widespread and destructive doorways is through drug use or drunkenness. Some drugs such as crack cocaine and methamphetamine are also associated with hallucinations and paranoia and often result in savage crimes that can only be explained in terms of demonic action.

"Many times entryways are there because of knowing or unknowing sin such as resentment and bitterness. Just as often, things that happened to the person, such as abuse and trauma, created the conditions for entry. Perhaps ancestors were involved in the occult and brought a generational curse to bear.

"The core element of consent is knowing or unknowing disobedience to the written Word of God. This is why Paul writes *'study to show thyself approved'* (2 Tim. 2:15 KJV). Anything in us that resists obedience to God's law is a possible open door to oppression."

## Signs of Demonic Oppression

Don does not believe that demons *possess* believers but they can *oppress* them. "Demons fall into one of three categories—steal, kill, or destroy, and there can be more than one who is attacking.

Don says, "It can often be difficult to know if a symptom is something that is in the person's flesh or if it is a demonic power. There can be physical depression that is not a demon, then tormented depression that clearly is. There are mental illnesses that result from physical problems and some that are clearly demonic in nature. The telling sign is torment and anguish.

"There are at least sixty symptoms that can signal the presence of demonic oppression. The most common symptoms include irrational fears, anger, rejection, and sexual perversions. I would also include compulsive thoughts and behaviors, lying and desires to criticize others. Demons are all liars.

"Other signs include terrifying guilt and feeling that God will not forgive, revulsion against the Bible, a compulsion to blaspheme God, compulsive thoughts of suicide or murder, and hatred against others, particularly church or religious leaders.

"We have seen deliverance resolve nightmares that are horrific in nature, perverted sexual desires, questioning God's Word, rebellion and hatred of authority, fascination with the occult, criminal activity, poverty, and patterns of failure."

## Demons and Sickness

Although not all illnesses are caused by demons, Don reports that they can play a role in sickness and disorders of all types. "Fibromyalgia, restless legs, arthritis, colon problems, cancer, and almost every disease that can be named can often be healed through deliverance.

"One man called me and told me he had hepatitis C and only had a few years to live. I told him that demons are the source of that. He said 'I know it. I opened the door myself when I put the needles in my arm.' Telling him that all he had to lose was a couple of demons, he agreed to try deliverance.

"We addressed the doorways he had opened, and five demonic spirits were cast out. He has been back to the doctor two or three times for blood tests and the report is that he is cured. Hepatitis C is undetectable through his blood tests, and he has no symptoms.

"Demonic powers are particularly implicated in physical symptoms that appear suddenly with no reason, including migraine headaches, choking sensations, deep despondency, violent rage and uncontrollable anger, doubt of your salvation, doubt of God's love, and seizures."

## Justice in God's Courtroom

"God's system is fundamentally a legal one. Believers have legal rights because of the work of the Messiah, but they can knowingly or unknowingly compromise those rights.

"People often don't realize that the demons are governed by laws also. The permission or legal right that demons have to be present must be cancelled before the demons can be permanently expelled.

"When I prepare for a deliverance session, I visualize the process as a courtroom in which rights are exercised and enforced. I consider myself to be operating in the courtroom of the great God Jehovah. He is the Judge and Author of all truth and righteousness. The laws are the Words He has spoken. Whatever God says is law."

## The Truth Makes Us Free

"The foundation of this courtroom is truth. It is not power and it is not authority. It is the truth that makes us free. Demonic oppression causes us to believe a lie. All demons are liars. Their rights to us are gained and maintained through deception.

"An example of such deception would be if a believer thinks it is OK to hold on to anger, resentment, and bitterness, even though we are repeatedly commanded to forgive. This provides a wide-open gate for demons to walk into our lives.

"When we recognize any sin, we must immediately confess before the righteous judge, and we must receive forgiveness through the blood of Messiah Jesus. Once this is done, demons no longer have rights to oppress us.

"Confessing the sin cancels the demons' rights to be present and they can then be cast out by commanding them to go in the name of Jesus. Just getting rid of sin is not enough. The demon must specifically be cast out and commanded to go."

## The Believer's Defense Attorney

"When I do deliverance, I understand that I am part of God's law firm, and I represent the believer. I am the defense attorney for the believer, defending and protecting the person's rights in the name of Jesus.

"I challenge the demons directly. I ask the demon to state his name and occupation. Jesus did this in Gadara when He said, '*What is your name?*' Demons have personalities, rank, and particular functions—to steal, kill, and destroy.

"Then I ask the demon if he has any legal right to remain in this person's life. If their answer is no, then we have absolute authority in the name of Jesus Christ to cast these demons from the individual and into the abyss."

## God's Angels—the Bailiffs

"God's holy angels are always present at these hearings and act as bailiffs to enforce God's commands and to minister to the believer.

"There is always victory in the courtroom when righteous justice is the goal of the believer. This justice means the desire to be free from any lies of the demons, not having any secret deals with the enemy, and not participating in any opposition to God.

"One important thing we stress is that deliverance is not for unbelievers. They must be saved first. God's system is fundamentally a legal one, and a person must be a believer in the Messiah to have rights."

# I Met the Son of Sam Serial Killer

David Berkowitz, the notorious serial killer known as the Son of Sam, was in a prison in New York. Don wrote him a letter in 1978, shortly after he had been sentenced: "I had seen people saved in prison so I wrote him a letter where he was in Attica, New York, that said 'God still loves you and Jesus can save you.' He wrote me right back and said 'Don't send me any more stuff like this. If I ever get out of here I will kill you.'

"About twelve years later, I was ministering in his prison, not knowing he was there. After the service, a man came up to me. Putting his arm around me, he said, 'I want you to know that I appreciate you being faithful all these years coming into these dark places with the light of the Gospel. By the way, my name is David Berkowitz.'

"I could tell something had happened by the look in his eyes. I said, 'David, are you saved?' And he said, 'Yes sir, I was born again a couple of years ago.' He said no one knew his story because the media would just twist it. After many years of friendship, David asked me to write a young man in an Irish prison. New York inmates are not allowed to write other inmates.

"David had read about Eddie Ferncombe, a violent youth who had stabbed 15 people by the time he was 15 years old. David asked me to write to one of the most hardened prisoners in Ireland."

# One of Ireland's Most Violent Criminals

"Eddie Ferncombe was a gang leader, a heroin addict, and a notorious, feared criminal. He wound up in Ireland's worst prison in maximum security, down in the dungeon.

"I wrote to him, and over a period of several weeks of writing, Eddie accepted Jesus. Eddie asked me for some tapes of my services. He wrote me a few weeks later after receiving them.

"On one of the tapes I had done a mass deliverance. On the tape I had said '...silently address those issues in your mind and choose to be set free from them. I bind every demon....'

"Eddie wrote me that he had had a strong physical reaction to this command. He began trembling and sweating and could not sit still. He became so hot that he had to splash water on his face, even though it was the middle of winter and very cold. He said 'I know I have demons! I told my chaplain about it. The chaplain laughed at me.' Then Eddie asked me to come to Ireland to help him be set free.

"I felt God's Spirit telling me to go, and things fell into place with the arrangements. I went to Port Laoise, Ireland, near Dublin, to one of the darkest, harshest prisons I had ever been in. I met with Eddie. I sat in a private visiting room with him—the shackles were removed as the officers brought him into the room.

HIS STRONGHOLD WAS UNFORGIVENESS.
HE COULD NOT FORGIVE.

"We talked about the doorways that demons could enter. His stronghold was unforgiveness. He could not forgive. I told him, 'You cannot have any unforgiveness in your life if you want to get rid of demons. I can't help you unless you forgive.'

"He said, 'I can't do that—as soon as I get out of here, I'm going to kill the man who snitched on me. I'm not going to forgive him.' I said, 'Then I can't help you if you won't forgive.' I left him to think it over and told him I would be back.

"I came back two days later. We were in a super-isolation area. He was escorted by four officers and had waist chains, ankle chains, and handcuffs. But he had a big smile on his face. He said, 'I did it, Brother Don. I forgave that man.'

"I could see in his eyes that it was real. We went through the process of binding demons and commanding them to leave and they did. Eddie has been out of prison now for six years."

## Eddie's New Sense of Freedom

Eddie was recently interviewed by telephone on the Messianic Vision radio program.[1] He was asked what it was like to be set free of evil spirits.

Eddie replied, "I was on a road to destruction. Inwardly I was in torment. I was very violent and very evil. I was in a very bad place mentally.

"After I went through deliverance, I felt amazing peace. The peace came straight away. After the deliverance all the darkness just lifted and I felt giddy and happy in my spirit. It felt better than being stoned!"

Eddie was in the worst prison of all prisons, hating and just wanting to get out to murder another person. Now he feels the love of God. God is so good. When people are freed from bondage, they feel wonderful.

# How You Can Be Free

"Jesus said cast out the spirits, but He also said the truth will make you free. So we understand that deliverance is never a power encounter. It is a *truth* encounter. When we have repented and received forgiveness, deliverance is a simple matter. There are four principles involved:

1. **Consent.** Either you have demons or you don't. If you do have them, it must be that there is some kind of permission for the demon to be there. The concept of legal permission is important and this consent must be removed.

2. **Commitment.** The believer must have a sincere desire to be free from demonic powers. The person's will is paramount in confession, denunciation, renunciation, and repentance. For deliverance to occur, the believer must truly want to be free. They must be willing to bring their lives into obedience of God's Word.

   "Every spirit in Heaven and earth must bow to the will of God, except one—the human spirit alone has the power to choose to disobey God. The human spirit can bow or not bow to the name of Jesus. If the person does not want deliverance, it will not happen.

3. **Cancellation.** There is no permission that cannot be cancelled. Once a person is willing to confess and repent of a particular doorway, he or she brings their life into obedience to the Word. Coming into agreement and obedience with God's Word can cancel any legal permission demons have. Jesus paid the price for us. His blood covers everything.

4. **Command.** When those legal consents have been cancelled, you must command the demon spirits within you to leave. You may carry sin for a period of time and then may repent. But when you repent, the demons do not necessarily leave until they are actively cast out.

"I've had demons, when I command them to leave someone, say that no one ever told them to go. They become like squatters, staying on even after the person has repented or forgiven. The demon hangs on because no one ever told him to go."

## Closing Thoughts

"If you suspect that demons are in some way oppressing you, study and come to a scriptural understanding of demons. This is the first step toward release.

"Make sure that you sincerely desire to be free, and will make no compromises or hold back. Determine to be free no matter how strong the demon's grip. Your will is paramount and you must be 100 percent committed to freedom.

"Ask the Holy Spirit to reveal areas of demonic bondage or torment and to reveal to you any possible doorways through your own life or through your ancestors.

"Associate deliverance with Jesus and freedom. Exercise your faith and understand God's unsurpassable gift to you in Jesus. The name of Jesus has absolute authority *every time*. When the consent or legal right has been removed, the demons can be cast out in Jesus Christ's name."

\* \* \*

For further study, read Don's book *When Pigs Move In*. For more information about Pastor Don Dickerman and his ministry, visit his Website at www.dondickerman.com.

## Endnote

1. To listen online to the radio program and learn more about supernatural healings, visit: http://www.sidroth.org.

Chapter 8

# The Messiah's Healing Light
## *Katie Souza*

*In Him was life, and the life was the light of men* (John 1:4).

The Scriptures promise that any believer can walk in the same power and glory for healing that Jesus had, but there is often a gap between the promise and our experience. Katie Souza found some of the missing keys to this promise for healing.

Katie discovered that we often do not understand the real cause of our problems, and do not appreciate the power of Jesus' glory light to heal inner wounds and forgotten sins. She teaches people how to apply the glory light of Jesus for complete healing. Katie has overcome tremendous obstacles herself as she learned this.

## Bonnie and Clyde Rolled Into One

The Scriptures say that to the person who is forgiven much, he will love much. Katie is just such a person. Before she gave her life to the Messiah, she was a real outlaw, a Bonnie and Clyde type of character.

Katie had gone to Hollywood with dreams of becoming a star, and had some early successes in film, television, and commercials. However, as her career started taking off, so did her illegal drug use. She became so heavily involved with drugs that she lost her movie career and descended into dealing drugs for a living.

As a drug dealer, Katie lived an outlaw life. She was known as a methamphetamine producer. She routinely stole cars to house her portable meth lab, and running from the police in high-speed car chases was a regular occurrence. When customers failed to pay her bill, she used guns, theft, and threats of violence to force them to pay. Before she was finally caught, Katie had racked up over a dozen criminal charges.

## WHEN CUSTOMERS FAILED TO PAY, SHE USED GUNS, THEFT, AND THREATS OF VIOLENCE TO FORCE PAYMENT.

Katie succeeded in eluding police for many years, but in 1999 she was caught and forced to pay the piper. Leading up to that time, she had gone into the hills in New Mexico to a house that was used for cooking methamphetamine. This house was drenched with so much meth contamination that the chemical residue on the floor melted her boots. The toxic fumes in the house were very strong, and she began to feel terribly ill.

Just when she was realizing that she should not be in that place, federal marshals surrounded the house, and took Katie into custody. But she was so sick from the meth fumes, they had to take her to a hospital for treatment.

# Katie Is Arrested by the Holy Spirit

When Katie regained consciousness, she was in a hospital, guarded by a federal marshal. Seeing an opportunity to escape, she hurriedly put on clothes and fled. However, as soon as she got outside the hospital, the Holy Spirit seized her and held her captive.

She describes what happened next: "I suddenly felt paralyzed. I kept trying to propel my body forward but it wouldn't obey. I went back into the hospital and started walking down the hall directly toward the agent. 'What am I doing?' I thought, panic-stricken, but I could not stop myself. Voices in my head now began screaming violently at me to turn back around, but something stronger wouldn't let me. Finally, I was standing directly behind my captor, yet neither he nor the nurse seemed aware of my presence. 'You can still escape!' the voices said. 'Turn around—it's not too late!'

"But instead of fleeing, I reached out my hand and touched the agent on the shoulder. Now I was committed. Startled, he turned around. When he saw me, he instantly paled. I saw pure fear in his eyes as a thousand questions about where I came from invaded his mind. The officer knew something had almost gone terribly wrong so he quickly put handcuffs on me, and that ended my chance to escape. I was eventually tried, convicted, and sentenced to almost thirteen years in a federal prison.

INSTEAD OF FLEEING, I REACHED OUT
MY HAND AND TOUCHED THE AGENT
ON THE SHOULDER.

"During my first year in prison, I was fighting with the guards and other inmates continuously and was in and out of lockdown seven or eight times. I was one of their most difficult inmates. One day I found out that one of my codefendants was going to testify against me, so I attacked her in the yard. They put me in lockdown again, but this time something different happened.

"I was sitting on the floor of a cold cell that smelled of urine and vomit. My back was literally against the wall, and I was feeling pretty miserable when I got a revelation—'This is God's way of dealing with you! It took this level of lockdown to get you to break.'

"I remember slumping back against that cold cement wall, thinking, *I can't do this anymore.* I had been fighting everybody out on the streets, and now I'm fighting everybody inside. I didn't even realize I was fighting God Himself. Right then, the Lord spoke to me, saying, 'I want you to surrender to your captivity, because this is My perfect plan for your life!'"

## Focusing on the Lord Changes Everything

Katie knew that God was talking to her, and she surrendered her life to Him. "Once I started to focus on the Lord, everything turned around. I began reading the Bible and I thought it was the coolest thing I'd ever read in my life. I would go from the front to the back over and over again.

"As I read, the Holy Spirit began to point out the Scriptures about ancient Israelites who went to prison. I was thinking, 'Wow, this is my story. It's the story of every con I'd ever known. I started getting excited about it, and I started teaching it to everyone who would listen.

"Everything began to change. The guards started calling our unit the 'God Pod,' because everybody was worshiping God. We were baptizing people in the shower and praying. There was fellowship going on, and an amazing breakout of the presence of God—right in the middle of our captivity.

"Instead of a punishment, captivity became the very ground on which God established a relationship with me. It turned me around and turned every fiber of my being to God. Prison makes you silent and sequestered so God can fill you up with His goodies.

"People are wrong to dismiss jailhouse conversions. In First Kings 8, I read that Solomon prayed that the people who went into captivity in Babylon would seek God with all their heart. So getting saved in prison is totally biblical.

"While inside I began getting revelation about the captivities of ancient Israel and I began to teach it to others. After a couple of years inside, God spoke to me and told me He was going to do a jail-break and get me out of prison. He even told me the exact date I would be let out. The next day I told everyone in the facility.

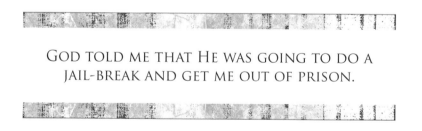

GOD TOLD ME THAT HE WAS GOING TO DO A
JAIL-BREAK AND GET ME OUT OF PRISON.

"By the end of the day, 1,200 women were laughing at me. When my counselor found out I was claiming to hear the voice of God, she sent me to the facility psychiatrist. The psychiatrist thought I had lost my mind and wanted to put me in suicide watch! But six months later I won a case in federal court. They took seven years off my sentence and the exact date the Lord gave me came to pass! It was such a powerful miracle that it caused people in the prison to be awestruck by God, His goodness and His power."

# Anointed for Healing

"God allowed me to be part of many healing miracles in prison. When I got out, I was praying for it to continue. Two years after I got out, God told me to go to Bethel Church pastored by Bill Johnson in Redding, California. He said if I went there I would receive an anointing to heal the sick, as it says in Matthew:

> *And when He had called His twelve disciples to Him, He gave them power over unclean spirits, to cast them out, and to heal all kinds of sickness and all kinds of disease* (Matthew 10:1).

"I was totally excited about this anointing because my mother was ill with a disease that was eating her bones, leaving her extremely crippled and in a great deal of pain. I felt this could be the breakthrough I was waiting for.

"On my second day at Bethel Church, I was standing in front of the church and two housewives with kids hanging on their skirts came over and laid hands on me to receive this anointing. I had a sense of liquid pouring over me; the power of God was filling me up. I knew that I had received the Matthew 10 anointing that allows you to cast out demons and lay hands on the sick. God did just what He had said He was going to do."

# A Power Generator Turned On

"I knew God had given me something special. Suddenly I had a switch that turned on a power generator inside me. As I prayed, heat and power flowed through my body and were released down my arms and out through my hands. I could not wait to get home to pray for my mother who had been in agony for twenty-five years from that terrible bone disease.

"I believed that Mom would be totally healed, but when I laid hands on her, I felt the power but nothing happened. Nothing happened for three days, although I kept praying. On the third day I prayed for my father who had been scheduled for prostate surgery and he was instantly healed. So I knew I had the power, but Mom had something that was blocking her healing from manifesting."

## An Order of Battle

"As I waited before God to understand this, the Lord explained Matthew 10:1 to me: *'Notice the order in which Jesus gave this to His disciples. He gave anointing to **first** drive out demons and **then** heal sickness.'* Casting out of demons is mentioned before laying hands on the sick. God showed me that sometimes before you can get rid of a sickness you have to drive out the demon that is causing the problem.

"I started rebuking demons for my Mom. I rebuked every demon I could think of and nothing happened. Then God told me that I was fighting the demons in the wrong order. There is an order in the demonic kingdom, like there are ranks in an army. That's why the wild man at the tombs said, *'My name is Legion'* (Mark 5:9). The word *legion* is a Roman army term. That spirit knew he was part of an army.

"In every army there are ranks including generals, colonels, sergeants, etc. God told me to stop fighting from the bottom up but rather work from the top down. He reminded me of the Scripture where Jesus says:

*No one can enter a strong man's house and plunder his goods, unless he first binds the strong man. And then he will plunder his house* (Mark 3:27).

"In Ephesians 6, I saw the order in which the demonic kingdom operated. The passage says:

*For we are not wrestling with flesh and blood [contending only with physical opponents], but against the despotisms, against the powers, against [the master spirits who are] the world rulers of this present darkness, against the spirit forces of wickedness in the heavenly (supernatural) sphere* (Ephesians 6:12 AMP).

"I could see this is the order to fight in the battle. Highest in the ranks is a despot, which is a tyrant king. No king is really a king unless he has a kingdom. In his kingdom are the powers and master spirits, the next two ranks mentioned in the passage.

"The despot kings are the rulers, and the next level down is the powers. The word *powers* actually means "orders of angels" and refers to the various ranks of fallen angels in the demonic army. The last level is the master spirits. The word *master* means to be able to control someone. These spirits have the ability to harm or manipulate us in some way."

## Fight the Demonic From the Top Down

"When I got the revelation of the order of the demonic kingdom, the Lord said that if I would learn how to defeat the kings, the powers and spirits would readily submit to me. If we fight the demonic kingdom from the top down, we will be successful.

"The story of David and Goliath demonstrates this. In this story, Goliath came every day to challenge the Israelite army. He said, *'Choose a man for yourselves, and let him come down to me. If he is able to fight with me and kill me, then we* [meaning me and my army] *will be your servants'* (1 Sam. 17:8-9). And that is exactly what happened. After David defeated Goliath, the Scripture says that when the Philistines saw their champion was dead, they fled without a fight! Think about that—if you defeat the champion, the entire army will back off!

"Jesus did this in the very beginning of His ministry when He was tempted by the devil in the desert. When Jesus was in the desert, the devil took Him up on a high mountain and said, *'Let me show you my kingdoms*—plural. *'If you will do homage to me I will give you these kingdoms'* (see Luke 4:5-6).

"When satan was offering Jesus his kingdoms he was not talking about cities like Jerusalem but rather places in the earth where his demonic kings were in positions of spiritual power. Jesus did not bow His knee to satan by worshiping him but rather Jesus took dominion over him, thereby taking power over every single demonic king in the dark realm.

"Immediately after that, Jesus began His earthly ministry. From that point on, every power and master spirit submitted to Jesus without a fight. Why? Because it was just like when David defeated Goliath. When the Philistines saw their champion was dead, they fled. Every power that Jesus subsequently came up against submitted to Him without a fight because He had first taken out the kings! He followed the right order."

## The Satanic King of Babylon

"I asked God to show me which kings had power over Mom so I could take them out, and He directed me to read Isaiah 14. Sure enough, the chapter was about a king, the satanic king of Babylon.

"In the natural, the king of Babylon took the Israelites into *physical* captivity. In the supernatural realm the satanic king of Babylon has the same job. He physically imprisons God's people by taking them into physical captivity by sickness and disease.

"Isaiah 14 in the Amplified version of the Bible tells us what his assignment is against us. He causes us *'pain,'* He *'weakens us and even lays us prostrate'*—all things that talk about afflicting the physical body.

"I began to make war with this king for Mom. At first I didn't know what to do, but I had the most important thing—the Scriptures. Our power is in the Word of God. Ephesians 6:17 calls it the sword of the

Spirit. I saw that Isaiah 14 says I could take up a taunt against him that would cause him to fall from his position of power in the second heavens. So I began to fiercely decree that Scripture against him.

"As I fought him I felt burning in my legs, power moving through my stomach. I continued to quote these Scriptures until I had an open vision in which I saw something like a man falling from the second heavens down to the earth.

## AS SOON AS WE DETHRONED THIS DEMONIC KING, ALL KINDS OF MIRACLES BROKE OUT AND MANY RECEIVED HEALING.

"He was screaming and I said, 'What was that, Lord?' Instantly, the Lord brought to me the Scripture about the time Jesus sent out the seventy-two disciples with the same Matthew 10 anointing I had received at Bethel. When they returned, they said even the demons submitted to them in His name. And Jesus said, *'I saw Satan **fall like lightning from heaven'*** (Luke 10:18). As soon as we dethroned this demonic king, all kinds of miracles broke out and many received healing.

"First, Mom was delivered from addiction to prescription pain medicine she had been taking for ten years. Then miracles began to break out for other people as soon as we removed the Babylonian king off of their bodies.

"Other drug deliverance miracles happened. A man was in such severe heroin withdrawal that his face was gray. Sweat was literally pouring out of his body. He was instantly delivered of the withdrawal when we broke the kings off him.

"A woman was having severe alcohol withdrawal. She was suffering with non-stop vomiting and diarrhea. When I started praying, her skin was bright red and hot with fever. I removed the king off her, and within less than a minute her skin tone returned to normal. The fever was broken and the vomiting and diarrhea stopped.

"People with viruses started getting instantly healed when we removed the Babylonian king off of them. Even a man who had an incision infected with puss got a miracle. When we broke the king off him and commanded the puss to die, his hand got hot and the puss disappeared. The next day the doctor declared that his incision was perfectly healthy.

"There was a woman who suffered with severe body pain for years. She felt like killing herself because it was so intense. She had many people praying for her, but had not received a breakthrough. Isaiah 14 says that the Babylonian king causes us pain. I drove the demonic king of Babylon off of her and commanded her body to be well. At first nothing happened, but three days later she woke up and she was healed.

"About six months later, I was in Australia. The Lord instructed me to send glory and light to one of Mom's hips. Her disease was causing her pelvic bone to get so thin that her leg bone was about to break through into her intestines. After I began to release light to her, I called and she told me she saw an angel repeatedly come into her room and beam light on her.

"At one point I felt like that pelvic bone was restored but then the Lord told me that Mom's leg bone was not properly seated in the hip joint and that I would need to command the two to come together, bone to its bone. When He said this, I heard the word 'thundering.' When I looked it up in the Bible, I discovered it was from Ezekiel 37:7 which says, *'So I prophesied as I was commanded; and as I prophesied, there was a [thundering] noise and behold, a shaking and trembling and a rattling, and the **bones came together, bone to its bone'** (AMP).

"As I read the Scripture, faith exploded in my heart. I flew home, marched right into her room and commanded her bones to come together. All of a sudden Mom said, 'Ouch! I got a pain!' When I asked her what she felt, she said, 'Well, it wasn't really a pain, it felt more like when the ball of a truck goes into the hitch of a trailer!' Her leg popped into the hip socket without anyone touching it!"

## A 'Jesus Fast' Led to Breakthroughs

"There is more to healing—there are missing revelations. As long as everyone, every believer, is not receiving perfect healing, we are missing something. God spoke to me and said, 'If You want to have dominion over demonic kings, you must become a carrier of Jesus because He is the King of kings. If you want to carry more light, then you need to carry more of Jesus because He is the Light.' Basically, if you want to see more healing, you need to get more of Jesus.

"Our entire team went on a 'Jesus fast.' We did not fast on food, but on distractions from Jesus. We read prophecies, prayed, and meditated on Jesus. We concentrated on listening to His voice, and spent a lot of time in praise and worship of Him so we could carry His presence.

"Since that time we have had mass deliverances and breakouts of supernatural healing in our meetings. People just sitting in their seats are getting healed, demonic powers are being broken off, pain and viruses leave, and bipolar disorders are being healed.

"We have an especially strong anointing for healing of mental disorders and things that are attached to the brain. One of my favorite Scriptures is:

> But unto you who revere and worshipfully fear My name shall the Sun of Righteousness arise with healing in His wings and His beams... (Malachi 4:2 AMP).

"In this passage, the word for healing in Hebrew is *marpe,* a word that also means to be sound of mind."

## Healing Gifts Belong to All Believers

Katie teaches that the healing gift can be multiplied—it belongs to all believers—because God wants everyone to walk in this power. It is not about the person, it is about carrying Jesus.

Katie says, "It was during the Jesus fast that I got one of the most powerful revelations I ever received. The Lord showed me one reason that many do not receive healing. It is because of the wounds in their souls. Our souls are wounded by sin, either the sin that someone did to us or the sin we did ourselves.

"Even worse, because these soul wounds are created by sin, it gives the demonic an opening to torment us with mental and physical illnesses and even afflict our finances. Third John 1 says: *Beloved, I pray that you may prosper in all things and be in health, **just as your soul prospers*** (3 John 1:2).

"When the wounds in your soul get healed, then miracles will break out in your physical body and your finances.

"Remember that in John 14:30, Jesus says, '*...the prince (evil genius, ruler) of the world is coming. And **he has no claim on Me. [He has nothing in common with Me; there is nothing in Me that belongs to him, and he has no power over Me]*** '* (AMP). Jesus is saying, 'There is no sin in Me so there are no wounds in My soul created by sin, therefore the devil has no power over Me.'

"We can see proof of this in Mark 5. Jesus goes to Gadara and there He encounters a violent crazy man. The Bible says the man was possessed by a legion of demons and lived night and day among the tombs, cutting himself.

"The man ran up to Jesus saying, *'What have You to do with me, Jesus, Son of the Most High God? [What is there in common between us?] I solemnly implore you by God, do not begin to torment me!'* (Mark 5:7 AMP). Legion recognized that there was nothing in Jesus' soul that was in common with him, so he had no power to torment Jesus.

"When our souls are healed, we will have nothing in us that is in common with the kingdom of darkness, and demonic powers will have no right to torment us."

## Living Among the Tombs

"Now we must ask, how could the man from Gadara become so demonized that a legion of devils was in him? I looked up the Scripture and saw that it says three times that he 'lived among the tombs.'

"The word for tombs does not necessarily refer to graveyards. In the Greek it means to recall or bring to remembrance. So it could be a monument that is set up to cause a perpetual remembrance. A monument set up to cause your mind, will, and emotions to be perpetually affected by a horrible event that happened to you in the past is actually a wound in your soul.

"The demonized man lived among the tombs. He lived in memory of the events that wounded him; and because all soul wounds are created by sin, it gave the spirit of legion the legal right to afflict him.

"When we are healed from the soul wounds of our past, the monuments and strongholds are torn down. The light of Jesus can shine from our regenerated spirit to our souls, giving us an increase in our level of dominion and spiritual authority."

# Healing Soul Wounds Brings Dominion and Authority

"I myself have had a lot of soul wounds because I have done so many bad things. The more I get rid of them, the more authority and dominion I have. I am going to give you an example of how you can get rid of soul wounds, and how doing so will increase your level of dominion and authority.

"I was on a ministry tour about to go to speak at my first session. The night before, the Lord had given me a dream in which I was cooking methamphetamine in a laboratory. Now, I had not done that in over a decade, but I knew that Job 33 says that God shows us what is in our soul through dreams and visions. This made me believe that I still had a wound on my soul from the sin of cooking meth. So I lay down and focused the Glory-Light of Jesus on my soul to heal that wound.

"The Scriptures say that Jesus is the Light of the world and He came to bring Light, which is life. That word life in the Greek is the word *zoe*, and it refers to the soul. So I focused Jesus' Glory-Light on my soul. I concentrated on His glorious light.

"When my attention wavered, I brought it back. I dwelt on Scriptures that describe His light. I knew that the light was entering my soul because I could feel a release or a shifting inside, and in fifteen minutes I got that healing!

"Later, I went to the meeting and as I walked into the room where I was going to minister, I could smell in my spirit the chemicals used to cook methamphetamine. When I told the hostess, she informed me that the building had been previously used for manufacturing meth!

"What was happening? The Lord knew that in order for me to have complete dominion in that place I must have nothing in my soul that was in common with the demonic in that room. This is why He showed me the wound in my soul attached to the drugs. Because I got healed in my soul, I had a new level of authority, and signs and wonders broke out in the meeting."

## Body and Soul Are Connected

"When your soul is healed, you will receive a whole new level of dominion over the enemy. You can even get a breakthrough for your physical body. Remember that Third John 1:2 says, *'Beloved, I pray that you may prosper in all things and be in health, just as your soul prospers.'* When your soul is healed, then miracles will break out in your physical body.

"I went on a speaking tour to a state I had never visited. As soon as my plane landed, I felt violently sick with a high temperature, bladder infection, and yeast infection—so sick I could hardly think.

"By the suddenness and severity of the attack, I knew I had a wound inside my soul that gave me something in common with demonic powers of that region. This wound was giving the demonic powers the right to make me sick. I knew I had to get that wound healed before I could break off the sickness.

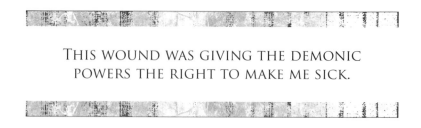

THIS WOUND WAS GIVING THE DEMONIC
POWERS THE RIGHT TO MAKE ME SICK.

"I asked the Holy Spirit to show me the soul wound that was opening the door to this attack. The Lord showed me five wounds in my soul that had been created by sin. I repented of those sins. Then I lay on my bed and opened my heart to focus on Jesus and His Glory-Light. As I did, I saw a vision of five wounded parts of me hiding in closets. I began leading them out into the light of Jesus and they were all instantly healed. Now I could command the sickness to leave.

"When I commanded the demonic spirit to come off of me, he actually yelled at me and said, 'What do you want?' He was so large his voice would have filled a two-story room. I said, 'In the name of Jesus, I want you to leave right now!' Immediately, I could feel it rip off my body and I was instantly healed. Again, my level of dominion and authority was increased, and amazing signs and wonders occurred at my next meeting."

## Position Yourself to Receive Healing

"In order to position yourself to receive healing, first ask the Holy Spirit to lead you in identifying the wound. Don't try to reason out what your wounds are. They are not always what you think. Sometimes what you think is the problem is really being caused by something else that is deeper. Let the Holy Spirit guide you by means of an inner sense, a memory, a dream, a vision, or even something someone says.

"Once you identify the wound, spend focused time repenting for the sins you committed that formed the wound. Also spend time forgiving someone who may have sinned against you and formed a wound in your soul. If you want to get a soul wound healed, you must first deal with the sin that caused it. Before you can apply the Glory-Light of Jesus on your soul, you must first repent and forgive in order to position yourself to receive healing.

"Wounds can be strong, blocking the desire for repentance, but you must do it. I knew a woman who had been molested by her father in front of her mother. She had a double betrayal to deal with, but she had to forgive them and repent of having developed bitterness. At first she could not accept this, saying she was an innocent child when they hurt her.

Eventually God sent her a vision of a light bulb in which the filament was broken. She realized that she had to forgive in order to let the light turn on in her soul."

## Use Faith and Focus to Receive Jesus' Glory-Light

"Once you repent or forgive, the next step is to focus on the Glory-Light of Jesus so that it can bring healing. A good example of this is in Numbers 21. In this story, the Israelites were traveling through the desert and the journey caused *their souls to become discouraged, and they spoke against God and Moses.* Because of their sin, God sent fiery serpents to bite them, and many of them died.

"What did they do to get the victory? The first thing they had to do was repent—they atoned for the sin that created the wounds in their souls.

"Next, they used faith and focus to get healed. They were told to *gaze steadily at a bronze serpent on a pole.* The Amplified Bible says that they were to look at it expectantly with a steady and absorbing gaze. Even if a serpent had bitten any man, he lived if he did this (see Num. 21:9).

"We know from other Scriptures that the serpent on the pole represents Jesus. Whether the Israelites understood it or not, they were being called to put their faith in Jesus to not only heal their physical bodies but also their souls. It was the wounds in their souls that got them into that situation in the first place!

"When we gaze steadily and expectantly at the Glory-Light of Jesus, we will be healed. Spend fifteen to twenty minutes twice a day contending to keep your focus on the light. If you get distracted, just return your gaze back to Him, looking steadily into His Glory-Light."

## Why the Glory-Light?

"Malachi 4:2 in the Amplified Bible says, *'But unto you who revere and worshipfully fear My name shall the Sun of Righteousness arise with healing in His wings and His beams....'* There is healing for your soul in Jesus' wings and beams of light.

"What do the wings stand for? The word wings is the Hebrew word *kanaph,* which stands for the corner of the prayer shawl. Jewish marriages are conducted under the prayer shawl because it represents the Israelites getting married to God under the pillar of glory cloud at Mount Horeb in the desert. So the wings represent the glory! That means Jesus arises with healing in His glory and His light.

"God's Glory-Light has the power to heal your soul. The best way to cause a huge light explosion in your soul is to get the glory to manifest through worship. The Scripture says that God's presence or His glory inhabits our praises. When you worship the Lord in a focused manner, giving Him all your thanksgiving and praise, His glory will manifest. When it does, you will experience an explosion of light.

"When Jesus was on the Mount of Transfiguration, a cloud of glory overshadowed Him. Matthew 17 says that the cloud was composed of light! If you will worship first, you will have access to more healing light than ever!"

## Soaking in the Light

"As the Lord brings memories to your awareness, you will apply the glory light to that memory until you are healed. Start with a positive expectation that Jesus has something for you in His Glory-Light. Look up Scriptures that pertain to Jesus and light—there are many of them—and meditate on them.

"In Revelation, John says the face of Jesus shines brighter than the noon-day sun, so you can imagine that picture in your mind. Meditate on these Scriptures. While you do, keep your mind focused. Let them come to life inside you in either words or images. Just soak in the light. Even try decreeing light Scriptures over yourself. Again, keep focused on His light while you do it.

"Soak in the light until you receive confirmation that the wound is healed. God will confirm it through things like Scripture, a dream, vision, or a *rhema* word. I remember the Lord woke me up one night to tell me I was molested as a child. I had no previous memory of it. I went through the steps of repentance and forgiveness. Then I started soaking the wound in His Glory-Light.

"On the third day of soaking, I stopped and asked God if the wound was healed yet. I got quiet and let God pop a Scripture into my mind. Instantly, I heard, 'Matthew 4:16.' I wasn't sure what that Scripture was, so I looked it up, *'The people who sat in darkness have seen a great light, and upon those who sat in the region and shadow of death Light has dawned.'* When I read it I knew I received my healing!

"Soak each wound until you get a confirmation. If bad memories or resentments come back, it is because the wound is still there. Just continue to soak. *When your soul wounds are healed, then you can command the demonic to come off of you!* There will be demonic powers attached to every soul wound. So make sure the final step you take is to rebuke the enemy in the name of Jesus!"

## Focus on the Glory-Light, Not the Wound

"The Lord may reveal to you some painful soul wounds through dreams or visions. Memories of old wounds can cause people to be bothered or depressed. It is very important that you do not let yourself be overly focused on the wound itself; the more you focus on the wound, the deeper it goes.

"God is showing you these things so that you will have a target on which to put His Glory-Light. Be joyful! When God shows you a wound, it means He is going to heal it. Just keep shifting your attention to the Glory-Light of Jesus and His willingness and ability to heal your soul. Look at the light expectantly. Focus your attention on His glory that is healing the wound, not the wound itself.

"As you diligently apply this, you will gradually become a being as Paul describes, *wholly filled and flooded with God Himself* (see Eph. 3:19 AMP). You will become as a lamp that shines its bright rays of light unto others. The whole point is to be so full of light yourself that you can bring healing light to others."

## Healing in the Light of Jesus

"There is healing in the Glory-Light of Jesus. You can meditate and decree these Scriptures over your soul:

*The Sun of Righteousness shall arise with healing in His wings* (Malachi 4:2).

*The people who sat in darkness have seen a great light, and upon those who sat in the region and shadow of death, Light has dawned* (Matthew 4:16).

*The lamp of the body is the eye. Therefore, when your eye is good, your whole body also is full of light. But when your eye is bad, your body also is full of darkness. Therefore take heed that the light which is in you is not darkness. If then your whole body is full of light, having no part dark, the whole body will be full of light, as when the bright shining of a lamp gives you light* (Luke 11:34-36).

*In Him was life, and the life was the light of men. And the light shines in the darkness, and the darkness did not comprehend it. [Jesus] was the true Light which gives light to every man coming into the world* (John 1:4-5,9).

*Then Jesus spoke to them again, saying, "I am the light of the world. He who follows Me shall not walk in darkness, but have the light of life"* (John 8:12).

*Then Jesus said to them, "A little while longer the light is with you. Walk while you have the light, lest darkness overtake you; he who walks in darkness does not know where he is going. While you have the light, believe in the light, that you may become sons of light…"* (John 12:35-36).

*The night is far spent, the day is at hand. Therefore let us cast off the works of darkness, and let us put on the armor of light* (Romans 13:12).

*For it is the God who commanded light to shine out of darkness, who has shone in our hearts to give the light of the knowledge of the glory of God in the face of Jesus Christ* (2 Corinthians 4:6).

*Giving thanks to the Father who has qualified us to be partakers of the inheritance of the saints in the light* (Colossians 1:12).

*You are all sons of light and sons of the day. We are not of the night nor of darkness* (1 Thessalonians 5:5).

*Every good gift and every perfect gift is from above, and comes down from the Father of lights, with whom there is no variation or shadow of turning* (James 1:17).

*And so we have the prophetic word confirmed, which you do well to heed as a light that shines in a dark place, until the day dawns and the morning star rises in your hearts* (2 Peter 1:19).

*This is the message which we have heard from Him and declare to you, that God is light and in Him is no darkness at all (1 John 1:5).*

*But if we walk in the light as He is in the light, we have fellowship with one another, and the blood of Jesus Christ His Son cleanses us from all sin (1 John 1:7).*

*Again, a new commandment I write to you, which thing is true in Him and in you, because the darkness is passing away, and the true light is already shining. He who says he is in the light, and hates his brother, is in darkness until now. He who loves his brother abides in the light, and there is no cause for stumbling in him (1 John 2:8-10).*

## There Is More You Can Do

"One amazing thing I have done from the beginning of my walk with God is to ask the Holy Spirit to give me a Scripture verse whenever I need the answer to a question. I will get quiet and let the Holy Spirit pop a verse into my mind. Then I go look it up, and almost every time it is an answer to what I was praying about.

"I have done this every day for years. Just get quiet in your mind, let the Lord speak a Scripture, for example, John 3:12, then read it. Sometimes you may hear a Scripture that does not exist. What that means is that you heard your own reasoning or God is not talking about that issue at that time.

"Jesus is the King of Glory, the King of kings. To get more healing, place more focused attention on Jesus. You can do this through worship music, fasting, Bible study, meditating on Scripture, and prayer. If you ask Him, the Holy Spirit will customize your Bible study about Jesus by putting specific Scriptures in your mind. This gives you a specific trail to follow in your pursuit of Jesus."

## Closing Thoughts

"Remember the lesson of Numbers 21—the Israelites had to gaze expectantly and attentively at the bronze serpent. Keep totally focused on Jesus. Decree the Scriptures over your soul. Keep applying the Glory-Light of Jesus to your soul. If you get distracted, come back to it as soon as you realize you have drifted away. It is OK to use your sanctified imagination—to imagine the radiant face of Jesus or the image of the Son of Righteousness arising with healing in His glorious wings. You can decree Scriptures over yourself. You can let the Holy Spirit send you a vision. The important thing is to focus in on Jesus, allowing His light to penetrate into you and do the work of healing.

"God's master plan is to bring Heaven and earth together. He wants His will to be done on earth as it is in Heaven. He has provided us with the tools we need to make this happen. The more we *get healed in our souls, the more we can be equipped to bring Heaven to earth.*"

* * *

Katie Souza has several teaching CD series and a book titled *The Captivity Series.* For more information about Katie Souza and her ministry, visit her Website at www.expectedendministries.com. You can also follow her on Twitter—details are on her Website at http://twitter.com/ ExpectedEnd.

# Chapter 9

# Soaking in God's Presence
## *Cindy Parton*

*Be still and know that I am God* (Psalm 46:10).

The realization that we actually have God within us can be life altering if we take the next step and learn to listen to Him and to experience His presence. Thanks to Cindy Parton, increasing numbers of people are learning how to listen to His voice within them. God has works for us to do that were prepared before we were born, and He wants to fill and equip us to do those works, as well as to give us times of refreshing and inner peace. We will always find grace and will often find healing, strength, and deliverance in His presence.

Cindy Parton has brought us an understanding of how to experience this intimacy with the Lord. She has developed a practice of consciously experiencing the presence of the Lord that she calls *soaking*. It is such a richly rewarding practice that thousands of people have come to her home to learn how to do it. They have taken it back to teach others, leading to soaking groups being formed all across the country.

In a radio interview for Messianic Vision,[1] Cindy said, "Any believer can *and should* experience the presence of God. All we have to do is ask Him to come, and then we wait. He always, always shows up, and always gives us what we need."

# A Special Delivery Message From God

I (Sid Roth) had heard that groups were getting together to experience God's presence, and that healing miracles were occurring in peoples' lives. So I visited Cindy's home in Texas, where it all started. There, I saw an amazing thing.

Cindy's living room was packed with people who had come to experience the presence of God. I found a remarkable sense of peace and pleasant anticipation. There was very little talking. These people were just sitting comfortably together in silence, with some worship music playing in the background.

Cindy prayed, telling the Lord how much we loved Him and asking Him to manifest His presence. After a few minutes, the power of God came on people. Some had visions, some had words of knowledge, and some were healed. Without exception, people were refreshed and encouraged. Everyone there experienced a touch of some kind from the Lord.

I had brought a staff member with me, and this young person had three separate visions during the meeting. In one of these visions, he was given a word from God for a specific individual whom he had never even met. The next day when we went out for dinner, we met a waiter who was the very person he had seen in his vision. I can tell you that this waiter was amazed and excited to get a special delivery message from God, and it was no less exciting for my staff member to be the messenger!

# Desperate for God's Real Presence

The idea for soaking meetings grew out of Cindy's determination to have greater intimacy with God. She describes it as follows: "About fourteen years ago I had reached a point where I was desperate for the real presence of God. I knew that He was a living God, and that one of His

Old Testament names can be translated as 'The Lord is Present.' I had even visited churches such as the Toronto Airport Christian Fellowship where His presence would come over the whole congregation.

"I also knew that I needed a living relationship with Him. I did not want to just hear about other peoples' encounters with God, I wanted Him to manifest Himself and be real to *me*. If we are going to reach the lost with salvation and healing, we have to be able to lead them into the life-giving presence of God. Just telling them about God and other peoples' experiences is not enough."

## God Is Present Where Two or More Are Gathered

"Matthew 18:20 says, *'Where two or three are gathered together in My name, there am I in the midst of them.'* My husband and I decided to make that a reality in our lives, and every night we began to gather in His name. We would sit down together and call out to the Lord. We invited Him to be present with us, and then we waited, and He did manifest Himself.

"We continued to do this night after night, and we found that He never disappointed us—He always came. We just basked in His presence, each time going deeper into the experience. It was so intimate and personal, touching us in ways that were always exactly what we needed. We found we did not need an agenda or a structure for this time. All we needed to do was just soak in the presence of the Holy Spirit."

## Sharing Our Experience

"My husband and I knew that this experience of the Lord's presence was something we were meant to share with others. So on Labor Day in 1995, we began to open our home to any who would come, and together we all soaked in God's presence.

"Gradually the number of people grew so large that sometimes there was scarcely room for everyone in our home. Eventually people started their own groups, and now there are many soaking groups across the country. The presence of God is so real and so life-changing, that once people experience it, they want to keep doing it and pass it on to others.

"This has been a labor of love. It is quite a serious commitment to have people in your home every week. And yet, it has always been a joy and a profound blessing to see God come and touch people and change their lives."

## The Spirit of God Is Within You

"Psalm 46:10 teaches us to '*Be still and know that I am God.*' That's what soaking is. We quiet our own mind and simply know that He is God. This takes us out of our concerns, and allows us to focus on the joy of His presence. The very act of stepping aside from your own concerns to be with God is an act of faith that creates inner healing.

"One person described it by saying, 'I was troubled about many things when I came. When I first started soaking, I felt huge waves of turmoil crashing over me as if I were on a beach. As I continued soaking in the presence of God, He took it all away. The waters calmed down. I saw myself running and jumping up and down and playing with the Lord just like I used to play with my dad. I just knew that I would be able to work through the things that were troubling me. The weight in my spirit lifted and I had a real sense of peace.'"

## The Soaking Experience

"In our soaking group we have a core group of people who meet beforehand to pray and intercede for those who are coming. We play some soft worship music, and as people arrive they quietly take their places and get settled. Some sit in chairs, others lie on the floor or however they feel best. I make available pillows and cushions and even light blankets because it is important to feel safe and physically comfortable.

"There is no agenda, and no plan. We just offer a simple prayer, telling the Holy Spirit how much we love Him, and asking Him to be present, and then He takes over. The most important thing is to let the Holy Spirit be in charge. He knows what we need.

"It can be difficult to let go of control, but we just need to be open to the Lord. It is so much fun because we never can predict what God is going to do. The one thing we *can* predict is that He will come, He will be present, He will do something that touches us, refreshes and renews us, and changes lives.

"After about an hour, the spirit lifts and then we draw into a circle to share what we all experienced. Sometimes people are given pictures, visions, a word of knowledge, a song, or even a poem. There is always a tremendous unity that has occurred in the spirit, and often people are given related experiences that are meant to work together. On one occasion when this happened, a woman had a vision of angels that ended in a paralyzed man, who had been a pastor, being completely healed."

## Pastor Healed of Paralysis

"This pastor had been in an auto accident that left him paralyzed from his chest down. His doctors had put him on disability and told him that he would never recover. Although he lived some distance away, he had heard about our meetings and wanted to come so badly that every week he drove several hours to attend.

"One night during the sharing period, a lady said that she had seen a vision of angels in our living room, ascending and descending a ladder into

Heaven. When she said that, something moved in the pastor's heart, and he asked, 'Where exactly did you see the ladder?' She pointed to a spot in the center of the room. He felt that he should just go and lay on the floor under the spot she had indicated.

"As he lay where the angels had been seen, the power of God came into Him. He was not completely healed instantly at that time, but the healing process began that night and from that point on, he began to see physical changes being manifested in his body. For the next several months, every time he soaked in the presence of God, he saw major improvement in his body, to the point that he went to his doctor and told him that he wanted to be removed from his disability status, and that he was going back to work. He even stood on his head to prove to the doctor that he had been healed!"

## Healing Takes Many Forms

Sometimes healing doesn't manifest right away the way we would like. Cindy herself went through breast cancer and is now a five-year survivor.

"I did hope that God would supernaturally heal me so that I would not have to go through surgery and chemotherapy, but that did not happen. I ultimately followed the doctor's plan, but I never had a moment of fear or anxiety. I had the peace of God the whole time, and never once had to cancel a soaking meeting in my home. Today I have a very strong ministry to women who are going through breast cancer."

## Each Time Is Unique

"Every soaking meeting is different from the one before. We never know what to expect, other than that He *will* come, and we *will* be blessed.

Sometimes people are given a song to sing, sometimes they dance, and on some occasions they laugh. Each person will react and respond differently when the power of God touches them, because He created all of us with different and unique personalities. When He comes, He gives complete and total freedom to all.

"Although each time is special in its own way, my favorite times are when His glory falls. At these times, there is a physical weight that we can feel pressing on us so that we are 'glued' to the floor. No one talks or moves, we just soak in His presence. No one wants to disturb what is happening or cause it to lift. This has been happening more and more frequently. The weight of His glory is something that everyone should hope to experience."

## Abiding in Him

In John 15:3-5, Jesus says that *we can do nothing unless we abide in Him*. He is the Vine and we are the branches. God wants us connected to Him so that we have the power to do His will. He is really saying that we must not try to live out of our own strength or understanding, but should be drawing our strength and our life from His presence.

By soaking in His presence, we develop an awareness of how the Lord communicates with us, and we gain the confidence to do the works He has prepared for us. As we spend time in His presence we develop this relationship.

## First Timers' Special Blessing

Cindy explains that "first timers" get a special blessing: "His power is so real that you can really feel His presence. Sometimes I have felt it flowing through me like a current. When that happens, I go around the room and lay hands on people so that they will get an infusion of this power. I have trained others to do this also. They go around the room, and as they are led by the Spirit, they touch people and impart a special blessing of the love of the Father. This helps people experience His love at deeper levels.

"This is particularly important for our newcomers. We call them first timers. We try to put the first timers in our center and give them an extra dose of the anointing. *It can take awhile to become conscious of His presence within us, but this consciousness is important if we hope to minister effectively to others.*

"I encourage people to receive in faith that God has touched them, even if they don't feel or see or think anything different. We cannot be in the presence of God and something *not* happen inside of us if we are totally surrendering everything to God and asking Him to come and change what needs to be changed in our lives—*To him who has, more is given.* Give thanks for what you do experience. A lot of times, God is working deep within us, beyond what we can perceive."

## Practicing the Presence of God

"When people first come for a soaking experience, they are often stressed or troubled by something. It takes a little time before they separate from all the junk that separates them from God. It is so important to know that God wants our full attention. *He wants us to want to be present with Him.*

"All we need to do is just wait on Him and trust Him to lead the time for us. There are no rules, no plans, and no agendas. All we need to do is have a pleasant expectation that He will be present. And whatever we experience, we should receive with a thankful heart. Many times people may feel disappointed that they did not have a fireworks type of experience, and this just is not right. God may need to work inwardly for a while before we can really recognize it. *So whatever you experience, receive it in good faith as God's gift and be thankful."*

## He Renews Our Strength

"The presence of God is exhilarating and refreshing. He always gives us what we need, whether it is a vision, a feeling of love, a word of guidance, or even a healing. As a grandmother, nothing gives me more pleasure than watching people enter into the presence of God and see their countenance change right before our eyes, and to watch how their lives are completely and radically changed for Jesus.

"Isaiah 40:31 says, *'Those who wait on the Lord shall renew their strength.'* As we soak in God's presence, we find inner healing. Our faith strengthens and our consciousness and ability to follow the leadership of the Holy Spirit increases."

## Nana-Fire

"One person whose strength was renewed is a special lady we call 'Nana-Fire.' She is a grandmother and retired registered nurse who had lost her husband after caring for him through a prolonged illness. When she first came to us, she was emotionally exhausted. She was depressed and lacked the desire to keep living. The first night she came she experienced a vision that has changed her life completely.

"In the vision she saw a dead plant sitting on a windowsill. She saw God run His finger around the rim of the pot. God told her, *'This plant represents you. Life will come back to the plant; it will be green once again and will live.'* Nana-Fire knew that the plant vision was life-giving to her. She caught the fire of the Spirit and was radically transformed.

"Nana now has a great sense of joy and vitality in living, and she has a wonderful gift for being able to impart this to others. It is really amazing. You see this little, sweet grandmother, but when she touches you, the fire goes through you and you have visions, dreams, and words from the Lord; that's why we call her Nana-Fire.

"Not long ago, Nana prayed for a man who suffered from diabetes and a seizure disorder. When she touched him, a surge of power shot through her arm down to her fingertips, healing the man instantly of both ailments. In that same meeting, she prayed for another lady who was also instantly healed of diabetes."

## Develop Your Gift

"Every one of us has gifts like this that we are meant to use for the good of the church. My husband and I are not conventional pastors. We are just ordinary working people. *There is no one who is too ordinary or too unimportant to be used by God.* He needs every one of us to get out there and work while there is still time.

"If you will take the time to soak in God's presence, I guarantee that He will come to you and fill you to overflowing. *It is up to you to get in God's presence and learn how to use your gifts.* He wants you to want to make time to be with Him.

"We all have differing gifts within us, gifts waiting to be activated, developed, and used. We can't use these gifts to minister effectively when we are hurt and wounded ourselves, so our first job is to get rid of our life hurts—to forgive and stop harboring anger, jealousy, resentment, and pride.

OUR FIRST JOB IS TO GET RID OF OUR LIFE
HURTS—TO FORGIVE AND STOP HARBORING
ANGER, JEALOUSY, RESENTMENT, AND PRIDE.

"I encourage people to minister out of their overflow of God's presence, not out of their own strength or a need to minister. We also must be able to let our guard down and to ask for prayer when we need it. It is not a sign of weakness to need prayer—it is a sign of strength to ask for it.

"Spiritual gifts are well-documented in the New Testament. Jesus says in Mark:

> *And these signs will follow **those who believe**: In My name they will cast out demons; they will speak with new tongues; they will take up serpents; and if they drink anything deadly, it will by no means hurt them; they will lay hands on the sick, and they will recover* (Mark 16:17-18).

"Each one of us is important in God's Kingdom, and we have a purpose in being here. We each have a gifting and calling and must learn to activate it and flow in it. By soaking in God's presence, we develop the ability to hear from God and act on it. We need to say to ourselves, 'God has given me this gift and I will learn to use it.'

"I encourage our group to 'practice' our gifts on each other. That takes the pressure off so we can learn how to flow into the ways that the Holy Spirit wants to use our gifts. It is the normal life for all believers to use their gifts on a daily basis."

# God's Preparation for What Is Coming

"The Lord is preparing His Bride, and in these days He is doing a new thing. The age of the church pastor doing all the work while the congregation sits passively are over. These are the days when each one of us should stir up our ministry gifts and get busy doing what God tells us to do.

"God is preparing His people for Heaven coming to the earth. He is getting us ready, giving us time to focus on others. It is time to start giving in to ministry that blesses others.

"There are so many frightened and hurt people who need the message about a living God who cares for them and who is able to heal and deliver. Psalm 37:9 says, *'For evildoers shall be cut off; but those who wait upon the Lord, they shall inherit the earth.'*"

# Closing Thoughts

"People come every week with a sense of awe, excitement, and expectation. It is never the same twice because God is always in charge. It is important to allow Him to be creative and to do the unexpected. It cannot be programmed. What is so amazing is that in His vast riches of blessing, everyone present has their need met, not just two or three people.

"Soaking is a wonderful opportunity for us to get our minds off our problems and focus on God. Just ask the Holy Spirit to come, and He will be faithful to do so. I describe soaking as immersing, saturating, being lost in the presence of God, being intimate with Him, recharging your batteries, and being full to overflowing.

"We all need the lasting change in our lives that can come only from being in the presence of God. People can do anything if God is with them.

Each of us is meant to be used by God; we don't have to be anyone special. The more humble we are, the easier it is."

## What You Can Do

Understand that God wants you to spend time alone with Him. Make an appointment to meet with God. Set aside a definite time, and put on some quiet worship music.

Begin with a prayer for the direction of the Holy Spirit and for His protection from other influences and distractions. Tell God you love Him and want to experience His presence. Then say, "Holy Spirit, come and do what You want to do." He will always come if you invite Him to come and make Him welcome.

Expect an encounter with the Lord, and be open to whatever the Holy Spirit decides to do. Do not try to impose an agenda or a plan on how things should go. Say a prayer of thanksgiving for whatever you receive, even if it was not a "fireworks" type of experience. Sometimes the quiet meetings are the most important.

If your thoughts are distracted by things you must remember to do, keep a notepad by your side and jot them down so that your mind will be free to move on.

IF YOU CARE ENOUGH TO KEEP A RECORD, GOD WILL BLESS YOU IN A SPECIAL WAY FOR BEING FAITHFUL TO RECORD THE EVENTS FROM THE HOLY SPIRIT.

Keep a journal or record of what happens each time. If you keep a record of what God is doing in your life, the things that He is showing you and speaking to you, you will be better able to see how God is working as time passes. I have also found that if you care enough to keep a record, God will bless you in a special way for being faithful to record the changes and events in your life from the Holy Spirit.

Make it a goal to spend time with Him, to get alone and be with Him. The more time you spend, the better you will know Him. Start with a few minutes, or whatever you can set aside, and do it as much in a group setting as possible so that you can practice your ministry gifts.

Learn to become a friend of God, and He will become your closest and dearest Friend. God takes care of His friends.

* * *

Cindy has been having soaking meetings for more than 14 years and she has learned what to do and what not to do. She has prepared a CD set with some guidance and a special CD with recorded music that was written especially for the soaking groups. For more information about Cindy Parton and her ministry, visit her Website at www.therivercenter.org.

# Endnote

1. To listen online to the radio program and learn more about supernatural healings, visit: http://www.sidroth.org.

# Chapter 10

# The Glory Realm
## *David Herzog*

*The earth will be filled with the knowledge of the glory of the Lord...* (Habakkuk 2:14).

A t a recent conference in Denver, a man stood up and told an amazed crowd that a ten-inch steel bar implanted in his right thigh had suddenly disappeared. He could no longer feel the rod with his hand, and the pain was gone. Others stood up and said they had also experienced sudden healing.

No one had prayed for these people as individuals, but the Spirit of the Lord was moving in the meeting, and miraculous things were happening. At the same meeting, a man with second degree burns on his body came into the building and was healed of those burns just as he walked through the foyer, before he even entered the conference room.

Welcome to the world of David Herzog. In speaking of this particular meeting, David said, "All through that conference people with various implanted rods and plates felt them disappear—but it was not anything I was doing. The heavens were open, and the glory of the Lord was present for everyone.

"We are entering a new phase in which the Lord's glory is literally invading the earth. When it is fully realized, it will usher in a supernatural acceleration of the things of God, and we will be able to challenge the very powers that hold back the advance of God's Kingdom. The Lord's Prayer says, 'Thy will be done on earth as it is in Heaven,' and that is just what we are seeing." (See Matthew 6:9-13.)

David's meetings are marked by outpourings of unusual signs such as instant weight loss, bald heads growing hair, missing teeth appearing or turning gold, and all kinds of healings and other creative miracles. David has seen dead people brought back to life, mass healings and deliverances, and has received accurate prophetic words. "This level in God is not due to anything special about me," David said. "It is for anyone who is able to discern the presence of the Holy Spirit, and speak out what he or she sees God doing."

God's call on David's life has taken him to minister all around the world, from the United States to India, the Middle East, Asia, and most places in between. He may stay and minister for a few days at a conference, or he may stay for months and preside over revival. The one constant is a manifestation of extraordinary signs and wonders.

## The Glory Realm

David Herzog has been praying for the sick ever since he was filled with the Holy Spirit during his teen years. As his ministry grew, he found he needed a new revelation about how to help people.

He said, "For years I ministered in a special gifting that I had for healing. I would pray for the sick, asking God to touch them, and good things would happen. But when you have been praying for hundreds of people, one on one, something comes out of you, and you feel a kind of weakness or a tiredness. I would sense that in God there had to be much more. How could I do even more in a shorter period of time?

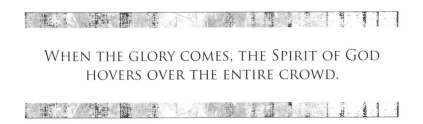

WHEN THE GLORY COMES, THE SPIRIT OF GOD
HOVERS OVER THE ENTIRE CROWD.

"I asked God how I was going to reach thousands of people at one time, or millions, and He introduced me to the glory realm. The glory realm is a time when *Heaven is open* to the people, and the Spirit of the Lord is present to do mighty works. It is like Acts 4:29 where Peter says, *'Now Lord, stretch forth your hand to heal.'* I realized that one moment under an open heaven would allow the glory to come down and touch a thousand times more people than I could in my own gifting and anointing, praying for individuals.

"When the glory comes, the Spirit of God hovers over the entire crowd. When I sense the glory of the Lord to be present, I can just speak one word and miracles happen instantly, not just for one person but for many, maybe even thousands of people. Marriages, finances, emotions—it can touch everything."

## The Glory Realm in Africa

"For example, I had a meeting in Africa, and the glory just came down from Heaven, and covered an entire stadium with thousands of people in it. While I was experiencing the presence of God's glory, God asked me, *'Now what do you see?'* I could see angels coming down and touching the people, and all I had to do was speak out what I was seeing for it to be manifested in the natural realm.

"I said, 'I see angels over here, I see angels over there.' As I gestured, masses of people fell to the ground, instantly delivered of demonic influence. It would normally take days and weeks to get all those people delivered of witchcraft.

"Instead of feeling drained, I was energized. I felt so light, and it was so easy.

"The same thing happens for healings and miracles as well. I will get a word of knowledge for weight loss, or for tumors, or for whatever, and the healing will come not just to one person, but thousands. That is the capability of God's glory."

## The Closest You Can Be to Heaven

"The Hebrew word for glory is *kavod*, meaning heaviness. To me the glory, the heaviness of the Holy Spirit, is the closest you can get to being in Heaven while living on the earth. It is breathing the rarefied air of Heaven. It is looking into the realm where anything you ask can be done on earth as it is in Heaven.

"In the Lord's Prayer, the Messiah says, *'Your kingdom come. ...on earth as it is in heaven'* (Matt. 6:10). It is not hard to figure out what is going on in Heaven. If you walked into Heaven right now, how long would it take to get a healing? It would be instant, no matter what your problem might be. That is what is supposed to be happening here in the earth. Body parts can be replaced, sight and hearing can be restored, marriages and finances can be healed—any miracle is possible.

"When we are in the glory realm, Heaven is open to us. The works of the Messiah to heal and deliver are accelerated, so that His will is done on earth as it is in Heaven.

"God lives in eternity, not in time, so whatever it is that you need, it is already done. You are walking into the *'It is finished'* realm (see John 19:30). If I start seeing body parts in the glory realm, I know that God has a creative miracle for someone, and all I have to do is call it out for that missing limb or blind eye to grow back."

# The Science of Creative Miracles

Although re-creating missing body parts would appear to violate basic laws of science, David provides an interesting explanation that shows how science and the Bible really do fit together:

"We are blessed to live in an age where science is beginning to catch up with the Bible. Nowhere in the Bible does it say that God made what exists out of nothing. It says that everything that can be seen was made by the Word of God together with things that cannot be seen:

> *By faith we understand that the worlds were framed by the word of God, so that the things which are seen were not made of things which are visible* (Hebrews 11:3).

"You have to wonder about those small particles, those things that cannot be seen. They appear to be the building blocks of creation and are key to understanding creative miracles."

## *Creation Is the Pattern for Miracles*

"The story of creation, laid out in Genesis 1, shows the pattern:

> *The earth was without form and an empty waste, and darkness was upon the face of the very great deep. The Spirit of God was moving (hovering, brooding) over the face of the waters. And God said, Let there be light; and there was light* (Genesis 1:2-3 AMP).

"Here we see that God's Spirit hovered over the face of the waters, and that God spoke to bring things into being. So we see two important ingredients, the Spirit of God hovering or brooding over the invisible things, and the act of God speaking them into being."

## *The Glory of God Works for You*

"The presence of God's Spirit combined with the act of speaking His will is a pattern that can be seen repeatedly through the Old Testament prophets. Elijah, for example, immersed himself in God's Spirit, and then called for rain to end a seven-year drought. God sent His Spirit, or His glory, first to hover, creating an atmosphere conducive to creative miracles. At the right time, Elijah spoke and rain was created (see 1 Kings 18:1,41).

*"God's Spirit hovering is the glory realm.* When you are in the glory realm, you are in the Spirit that is hovering over the people. And if you speak out what God is telling you or showing you, then things will be created at that moment.

"The key thing is to be aware of God's Spirit being present and take what action He shows or tells you to take. Sometimes people start declaring the prophetic word before the glory is full. At other times they sense the energy and power of the glory being present, but they don't see what it is doing, or what is supposed to happen so they fail to speak or perform what needs to be done. Both parts need to come together.

"The presence of God's glory is a perceptible weight or heaviness. It releases a supernatural energy and provides the potential for miracles. The glory of God is His presence, His Spirit, His power. The glory of God is not an emotion. It is a capacity for work—just like electricity and the sound waves that you can't see. Just as with electricity, you can be surrounded with it but if you do not know how to use it, it does you no good."

## *All Creation Can Respond*

"Some scientists believe that the smallest possible particle is not an atom or even an electron. They believe it is a vibrating fragment of energy called a string. They theorize that all that exists is made of these vibrating strings of energy.

"Because these little bits of energy vibrate, I like to think that this is sound energy in its smallest unit. If this is true, then every created thing can hear in a sense and respond in some way. All things created were first created with the same core ingredients—sound and the presence of God.

"God commands the sun, moon, stars, and other elements of creation to praise Him. He would not do this unless He recognized that all creation has the ability to hear, respond to, and worship its Creator. Jesus commanded the fig tree to die and the tree obeyed Him (see Matt. 21:18-19). Believers are commanded to preach the Good News, as everything can respond to the spoken word in the glory, including all of creation. Every living thing can and does respond to the Word of God even through you!"

## Sound Energy Has Real Power

"Many people who pray successfully against cancer speak to it directly and tell it to go away. Similarly, they may tell broken bones to be healed. It is possible to talk to sickness in this way because every thing living responds to words spoken in the Spirit and glory of God.

"Ezekiel prophesied to the dead bones, *'O dry bones, hear the word of the Lord!'* God told him to speak to the bones directly (see Ezek. 37:4-6). Bones can hear and respond to God's Word, just as all body parts do.

"The power of sound should not surprise anyone since ultrasound is used to both treat and diagnose various diseases including cancer. For example, high intensity sound waves—ultrasound—can be beamed at a tumor to destroy it. When you speak high intensity words powered by the glory of God's presence, you also are using sound waves to destroy a tumor.

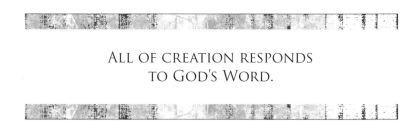

## ALL OF CREATION RESPONDS
## TO GOD'S WORD.

"All of creation responds to God's Word. Moses spoke to the rock and told it to produce water (see Num. 20:10-11). When satan tempted Jesus in the desert, he told Jesus to *'command that these stones become bread'* (see Matt. 4:3).

"In Matthew 17:20, Jesus said that we can speak to the mountain and tell it to move. In Luke 8:25 we see that the disciples marveled that *'even the winds and the waves and water...obey Him!'* All of creation can respond to you when you speak the words of faith, directed by God in the glory realm."

## She Spoke to the Bones Directly

David believes that when any believer gets an understanding or a revelation about the glory realm, he or she will be able to experience signs and wonders, angelic visitations, and other manifestations of the open heaven. He describes how easy it can be:

"A lady came to one of my conferences in California with a wonderful testimony. She had read my book, *Glory Invasion,* just before going to see her mother. Her mother had some kind of major physical injury, and she had to help her mother move about, clothe her, help her walk, and do all kinds of things for her.

"At first she prayed for her mother in the regular way, saying, 'O Lord, please help her. Please do a miracle!' But nothing happened.

"She started thinking about what she had read in my book and she realized, 'Wow, her body parts can actually hear me, they understand when I speak to them, just as David wrote in the book!' With this revelation, she applied what she had read, and she said, 'Bones, I know you can hear me now. In Jesus' name, bones come back into place!'

"The body parts began moving. Her mother said that she suddenly felt like a semi-truck had rammed into her side. Her entire hips and bone structure shifted into place, and she could walk.

"She was so excited as she shared in the meeting, telling everyone, 'I read the book and God used me to do a miracle!' That was more exciting for me than me seeing a miracle in my meetings—someone else having the joy of operating in the supernatural."

## You Can Enter the Glory Realm

"When the glory comes, we have to act, obey, and let God do as He intends to do. The first thing is to get the glory realm to open up. Of all the things that open the glory realm, the first and most important is holiness. The second is through praise and worship, followed by fasting with prayer, and sacrificial giving."

### *Holiness*

"Most of the great revivals of the past have started from a foundation of holiness, including repentance and forgiveness of sin. Your conscience coupled with diligent study of God's Word will give you an inner guide to holiness in your daily living. Pursue holiness so you can stay in the glory and keep the channels of intimacy with God open."

## *Praise and Worship*

"The Bible says that God is enthroned on the praises of His people, and many Old Testament prophets used music as a way to enter His presence. We are to praise and worship God, not because He needs our approval, but for what it does for us. It actually opens a portal into the glory realm.

"There is a pattern to praise and worship. When we follow this heavenly pattern, the glory realm opens up here in the earth. It consists of starting with high-energy praise songs—the kind that make you want to dance or shout to the Lord. This is what I call breakthrough praise. Basically you praise God with enthusiasm, or fast tempo songs, with all the passion of your heart until the Spirit of Worship comes, a slower, intimate time of worship.

"You will notice the Spirit of Worship coming because you no longer feel like shouting; you feel like telling God you love Him in the most beautiful manner that you can manage. The songs of worship are intimate and slow, like a caress or a loving kiss.

"As we lose ourselves in worship, we begin to sense the thick, heavy presence of God. This is His glory filling the room."

## *Fasting and Prayer*

"When you fast and pray, you are denying food in order to get more of God. This helps you break through into the glory realm at an accelerated pace. You can hear God better, and the power and presence of God increases upon you. You will be amazed at how much your faith will deepen if you are spending your fasting time in the Word and in prayer and praise."

## *Sacrificial Giving*

> *Now the multitude of those who believed were of one heart and one*
> *soul; neither did anyone say that any of the things he possessed was*
> *his own, but they had all things in common. ...Nor was there any-*
> *one among them who lacked; for all who were possessors of lands or*
> *houses sold them, and brought the proceeds of the things that were*
> *sold* (Acts 4:32-34).

"There are many examples in the Bible of people who were abundantly blessed when they gave sacrificially. One example is the widow who
gave her last meal to Elijah, and then saw her son raised from the dead (see
1 Kings 17:15-22). Another is Solomon sacrificially giving God a thousand animals on the altar causing the heavens to open and God asking him
what he wanted (see 1 Kings 4:29)."

## Portals

"As noted earlier, the glory is the capacity to do creative work. This
work can cover health, deliverance from demonic powers, weight loss, hair
growth, finances—everything that we could ever need. When the glory
comes, people are under an open heaven and miracles come easily.

"God wants to invade the earth with His glory, and He is revealing
places and times where this glory seems to cross over more easily. These
gateways between Heaven and earth are called portals.

"There are seasonal and geographic portals where His energy seems
to cross easily through an open heaven. The obvious geographic portals
include Jerusalem and Bethel, near Jerusalem, but there are others.

"These are places in Israel where you walk in, and instantly you can
be in the presence of God because the gateway is open. Take Bethel, for

example. The Bible says this is the gate of Heaven, and this is where Jacob camped and saw the angels (see Gen. 28:12).

"In addition to places, there are specific dates; I call them seasonal portals—seasons in time when the gateways open up. These are the feasts of Israel such as the Feast of Tabernacles, Shavuot, and Passover, that were ordained to be observed forever.

"These biblical feasts are divine appointments with God. Some people dismiss the feasts because they think they are just legalism of traditional observance, but God never changes. The presence of angels, the Spirit of God, the glory—are so much easier to experience during these appointed times."

## *Vision at Bethel*

"Of course, the best is to be in Israel at one of the portals during one of the feasts, because you are experiencing a seasonal portal and a geographic portal at the same time. So I took an unusual tour group to Bethel during the Feast of Tabernacles.

"To get to Bethel, we had to travel right past Ramallah via a bulletproof bus, and it took awhile to find the location of Jacob's well. When we settled down, it was dark. We began to worship the Lord. I told everyone, 'OK, just lie down and kind of relax, and see if God gives you a vision or an experience or something, because we are at both a seasonal and a geographic portal.'

"As I lay there, I was suddenly taken to an experience. I saw a sea of glass, and I saw the throne. I was taken right to Jesus. He looked at me and said: *'Thank you for coming and touching Isaac, my people. Now I am going to also send you Ishmael. You are going to touch Ishmael, the Arab people.'*

"Within a month I was in Dubai and Qatar, ministering to one of the sheiks. I got to pray with him, and his arm was healed. The word got around, and that night thousands of Muslims showed up at my meeting.

"People in the Middle East are not so much interested in philosophy as they are in miracles and signs before believing. God did signs and miracles for them in abundance. We had a man whose hair turned from white to black. A number of people who were bald had their hair grow back. Tumors were healed, all kinds of miracles happened. This drew large, large crowds and many were turned to Jesus."

## Great Acceleration in Israel

"It all fits together with the idea of *One New Man* in the Messiah. What a testimony it will be to the world when Arab and Jew stop fighting and worship the Lord together.

"We are entering a new season of great acceleration in Israel. Much spiritual activity will be occurring in the near future, and many in Israel will be open to the Messiah on a new level. There will be an increase in dreams and visions of the Messiah and a harvest that is riper than ever, both in Israel and among Jews in America.

"Keep your eyes open for divine appointments that will lead to awesome salvations among those you would normally consider the least open to the Gospel in times past.

"God is removing the veil in a big way as a new harvest is ripening. This applies not only to the Jewish people but also to many groups in deep darkness, such as those steeped in New Age and false religions and other power sources. Those in the entertainment industry, as well, will start seeing Saul-to-Paul types of transformations."

# One Way Into Heaven

"I live in Sedona, Arizona, where there is a lot of interest in New Age ideas. On one occasion, I went into a health food store to pick up a sandwich and visited briefly with a girl who was very much into Buddhism. She had been experimenting with levitating by means of inviting ten thousand Buddhas to come inside her. (This is a conversation you can only have in a place like Sedona.)

"I began to witness to her about Jesus, and she said, 'Oh, I love Jesus, too. He's so great, and He's my friend.' I told her that He died for her, and that He rose from the dead. Then she said, 'Oh, I can relate to that because I rose from the dead, too!' She told me that she had been clinically dead in the hospital, and that Jesus appeared to her, and she came back to life.

"She'd had no one to explain the salvation experience to her, so she was studying to be a psychic and learning to help people. She asked me if I could explain something to her. Following the ten thousand Buddha-demons experience, Jesus had appeared to her. He took her to a place called the Kingdom of Heaven, but for some reason she could not get in. And a voice said to her, *'No man comes to the Father but through Me!'* (see John 14:6). She had no idea what this meant.

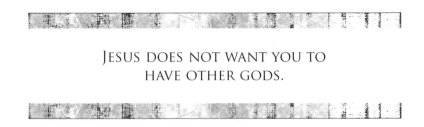

JESUS DOES NOT WANT YOU TO
HAVE OTHER GODS.

"I told her what it meant. 'Jesus does not want you to have other gods. He loves you and wants to be your only God. You should have no other lovers, no more demonic encounters. He is the only real God, and He loves you.'

"She felt the truth of what I was saying and began to weep and cry, so we were able to pray together right there. There are a lot of people in the occult and New Age who don't know about the Messiah. They are looking for something; they have a hunger for God. They are desperate and the counterfeits look really good until the authentic is shown to them.

"We are so blessed to live in a time when the authentic presence of God is being revealed, and it far surpasses any counterfeit!"

## You Can Enter the Glory Realm

Remember that creation itself began with the Spirit of God *hovering*. This is a very important truth to learn. When the Spirit of God is hovering over someone, the power of God is present, and the potential for miracles is present. Releasing the working of creative miracles must be done while His Spirit is hovering this way. It is a simple concept, but one that is easy to miss.

To enter the glory realm and see results, there has to be a coming together of what you *think*, what you *feel*, and what you *know* in your heart to be true. Things you can do to enter the glory realm include: personal holiness, prayer and fasting, praise and worship, and sacrificial giving.

Once you are in the glory realm, wait on God to move. Listen to Him and do only what you see Him do or hear Him tell you. Learn to hear the voice of God and be faithful to it.

While His Spirit hovered, God created by speaking. He spoke the world into existence. He used sound waves to make what exists, and everything in creation can respond to sound. You are made in the image of God, and speak on His behalf, declaring what He wants to do. For example, while the glory is hovering and you can hear His voice saying something like, *bones are being healed,* you must speak these words out, even if what you hear seems impossible.

## Get to Know Your Creator

A radical change is needed in the way we think about God. We are too much chained to the naturalistic way of thinking. When we expand our thinking to God's capabilities and comprehend the level of supernatural activity in the Bible, it is easy to see that the supernatural is waiting for us.

Jesus, Yeshua, the Son of God wants you to know the Creator of the universe. You know *about* Him; now He wants you to *know Him personally.* Everyone can see evidence that there is a Creator, but God wants you to know Him personally. Why? Because He loves you. He wants you to have intimacy with Him, and there is no other name given under Heaven in which we must be saved but the name of Yeshua, the name of Jesus.

God is so good; He really loves you. It is not an accident you are reading this right now.

* * *

For more information about David Herzog and his ministry, visit his Website at www.theGloryZone.org.

Chapter 11

# Your Next Step

## *Sid Roth*

M y prayer for you is that this book will help you take the next step in your own healing. God is just as willing to heal today as He was when Jesus walked the earth in bodily form. And He has given this gift to the body of believers. All believers should be able to pray effectively for healing, and to help others find healing as well.

How do you get to this point?

In closing, I would like to share with you some of what I have learned in more than 35 years of ministry.

## Ask the Holy Spirit to Flood You With His Presence

If you have repented of your sins, made Jesus your Lord, and asked Him to live inside of you, then you are a candidate to be baptized in the Holy Spirit. Ask the Holy Spirit to flood you with His presence. You will experience His presence more and more as you pray and worship God, especially if you pray in tongues.

## Pray in Supernatural Languages

Begin to worship God in a supernatural language—tongues. Speak out loud a language you have never been taught. If you are waiting to hear the language first, that is not faith. You will only hear it when you speak it out loud.

If you are thinking, "I don't know what to say," that's perfect! The language is not in your mind, but in your spirit. Your first syllables and words will sound unfamiliar and you will think you are making it up. But if you pray quickly, pray as fast as your tongue can move, you will do a mind "bypass," and an entire language will come out.

When we pray in tongues, our spirit prays perfect prayers. God knows our future, and we can pray away all demonic intervention. That is why Paul says in First Corinthians 14:18, *"I speak with tongues more than you all."* The gift of tongues is the doorway into the supernatural.

## Enter the Holy of Holies

If you are Spirit-filled, it's time for phase three. It's time to enter the Holy of Holies. But let me caution you. Before you enter, make sure you have repented for all known sin.

Start praying to enter the Holy of Holies. Start cultivating the presence of God 24/7. Live a life of praise and gratitude. Refuse to gossip or worry. Make sure you are not a divider of His Body. Spend time thanking God. Whenever I'm by myself, I am continually being thankful and praising Him and worshiping Him.

Read His Word regularly. Meditate on His promises of healing. Listen to anointed music, and soak in His presence. Simply stated, become normal from God's point of view. And get ready for a God encounter.

When the miracles start, always give *all* the glory to God!

## Learn the Way of Peace

Not too long ago, I was trying to go to sleep, but I was having a problem relaxing because a ferocious storm was raging outside my home. As I lay in bed, I kept thinking of the scene from Mark 4:38-39 where the disciples were also confronted by a storm.

They were in a boat, and it must have been really frightening for them to be in a small boat tossed by huge waves in the midst of a violent storm. However, Jesus was not afraid.

He was at such peace that he was sleeping! When they woke Him up, He took care of things but criticized them for worrying. We also can be at such peace in a storm by knowing that He will take care of it.

This has become my secret insomnia cure—lay down thinking about the storm Jesus was in. If He could have so much peace that He could sleep with the ship about to fall apart, then what have we got to worry about?

## A Place of Peace

I have learned something about peace that I wish I had known years ago. It is a powerful truth revealed in Mark 5:34. This is a beautiful story about a woman who was instantly healed of a bleeding disorder when she touched Jesus' clothes.

"...YOUR FAITH HAS MADE YOU WELL..."

Many were crowding against Jesus as He walked, but Jesus felt something when *she* touched Him. He felt virtue, power, go out of Him when she made that contact. So He stopped and asked the crowd, *"Who touched My clothes?"* (Mark 5:30). She came forward and told Him her story.

Now listen carefully to what He said, *"Daughter, your faith has made you well..."* (Mark 5:34).

He did not say it was her great need or God's great love that made her well. It was her *faith*—faith strong enough to pull power from Him when He was not even paying attention. This daughter's faith plugged into His power and she was healed.

## Go Into Peace and Be Continually Healed

Now look at what He says next, *"Go in peace, and be healed of your affliction"* (Mark 5:34). A more precise translation such as we find in Wuest and in the Amplified Bible says, *"Go **into** peace and be **continually** healed."*

There is a place and this place has a name and this place is called peace. If I can go into peace and not out of it, I will be continually healed of my affliction. I will be in a Sabbath rest, as we read in the Book of Hebrews.

## Enter Your Sabbath Rest

Sabbath rest is something that the ancient Jewish people understood well. God made the world in six days, and ceased from His activity on the seventh. Our Sabbath rest is when we cease from our striving. God is saying that *peace is a place* and we can go into it and be continually healed. There is a peace and Sabbath rest that we are to enter.

Peace is a place, a substance, and a realm. We can go into this realm and we can stay there, walking in humility, and living as a disciple of Jesus without strife and without stress. That is the kind of trust we are to have in Him.

It is my aim that we all walk into that peace. Most doctors will tell you that stress is involved in every illness. Peace is complete freedom from stress. Peace so radiates in your body that there is no room for stress, worry, or sickness. The Lord wants you to have that peace.

I am not there completely, but I want to dwell in God's peace. I know where to find it. I am learning to walk in another realm.

We can be in two places simultaneously. We are here and also seated in heavenly places. We can be here and in the heavenly realm at the same time.

## Hold on to Your Healing

There is one other nugget in this passage about the woman who had the bleeding disorder. When she touched Jesus, He stopped and looked around and said, "I felt virtue (healing power) go out of Me." He felt something go out of Himself.

I used to pray for my family members when I was a young believer. I would feel the virtue go out of me, and I would expect that they were healed, but they did not manifest their healing. I wondered what was wrong. Now I know.

The healing anointing went into them the moment it was released. They could have kept it if they had faith, because it takes faith to receive the healing. It is important to believe that you have received your healing and begin thanking God for it. If you don't acknowledge the anointing going into you, you are giving up on the medicine before it has a chance to work.

God does not live in time as we do. In the invisible realm there is no time, and healing is already done. When someone prays for you, you should be thanking God and going about your business.

The symptoms may still be there, but in the invisible world there is no time. Just thank God and continue cooperating with your medical doctors until your natural body catches up with your faith.

# Meditate on His Promises

Meditate on God's Word until it becomes real in your spirit. Meditate and talk about the promises of God until you have real, heartfelt, spiritual peace. You will know the truth and the truth will make you free.

Study the testimonies of those who have been healed. You can find many of them on my Website at www.SidRoth.org under the television and radio archives. You can also find them in the books we make available on the Website, and you can find them in the Bible.

As you meditate on the Word of God, you will automatically find your thought life moving away from fear. Fear is the opposite of faith. Fear is actually faith in a bad outcome.

Hebrews 4:12 says that the Word of God is a living thing. It is like a medicine. As you take this medicine continually throughout the day, you will find that not only does your faith grow, all kinds of negative thinking drops away. You will have peace and freedom from all kinds of stress. You will grow abundantly in your trust in God.

# Speak About the Promises

The Book of Revelation says something very important about healing. It says that the devil is overcome by two things:

1. The blood of the Lamb.

2. The word of the believers' testimony (see Rev. 12:11).

There is power in your words. Whether you speak about the promises of God or the miracles of Jesus from the Bible, your faith will grow exponentially.

As an added benefit, there is power in your testimony. It has been my observation that when people who are healed share their testimony, others are often healed of the same condition. This is also true when you share the testimonies of Jesus.

## Do Not Give Up

People most often do not manifest their healing because they give up. They expect it to be easy and instant, and fail to meditate on God's promises. They may fail to pray in tongues or cover their bases of unforgiveness. They may fail to recognize the role of hereditary curses or demonic oppression.

The truth is, you cannot lose if you do not give up. The Word of God is true, and you can rely on it and trust in Him.

## Peace. Be Still.

Fear may try to come in. Fear is a spirit. Fear is the opposite of faith. Fear says you are finished. Peace says "NO!" to the spirit of fear. Remember Jesus during that great windstorm in Mark 4:39. He was in the stern of the boat, sound asleep. When the disciples woke Him up, He said to the sea, *"Peace! Be still!"*

Jesus is the Prince of Peace, the Sar Shalom.

He is saying to you right now, *"Enter into My rest. It's a real place. Let's go there."*

\* \* \*

For more information about Sid Roth and his television and radio ministry, visit his Website at www.SidRoth.org.

WRITE FOR OUR
FREE NEWSLETTER
AND CATALOG:

# It's Supernatural!
## and
# Messianic Vision

P.O. Box 1918
Brunswick, GA 31512-1918

Telephone: 912-265-2500

Fax: 912-265-3735

Email: info@sidroth.org

Visit Sid's Website:
www.SidRoth.org

# CHECK SID'S SPEAKING ITINERARY.

Watch online or download archives of his TV show, *Its' Supernatural!* and his radio show, *Messianic Vision*—or subscribe to the podcasts!

Shop an online catalog jam-packed with mentoring tools and resource materials.

Enjoy a library of articles on topics such as Jewish roots, the One New Man, Israel updates, powerful prayer, supernatural healing and experiencing the presence of God, and much, much more!

Visit Sid's Website:
www.SidRoth.org

# In the right hands, This Book will Change Lives!

Most of the people who need this message will not be looking for this book. To change their lives, you need to put a copy of this book in their hands.

> *But others (seeds) fell into good ground, and brought forth fruit, some a hundred-fold, some sixty-fold, some thirty-fold* (Matthew 13:8).

Our ministry is constantly seeking methods to find the good ground, the people who need this anointed message to change their lives. Will you help us reach these people?

> *Remember this—a farmer who plants only a few seeds will get a small crop. But the one who plants generously will get a generous crop* (2 Corinthians 9:6).

## EXTEND THIS MINISTRY BY SOWING
### 3 BOOKS, 5 BOOKS, 10 BOOKS, **OR MORE TODAY,**
#### AND BECOME A LIFE CHANGER!

Thank you,

Don Nori Sr., Publisher
Destiny Image
Since 1982

# DESTINY IMAGE PUBLISHERS, INC.

*"Speaking to the Purposes of God for This Generation
and for the Generations to Come."*

## VISIT OUR NEW SITE HOME AT
### WWW.DESTINYIMAGE.COM

---

## FREE SUBSCRIPTION TO DI NEWSLETTER

Receive free unpublished articles by top DI authors, exclusive

discounts, and free downloads from our best and newest books.

**Visit www.destinyimage.com to subscribe.**

---

Write to:    Destiny Image

P.O. Box 310

Shippensburg, PA 17257-0310

Call:    1-800-722-6774

Email:    orders@destinyimage.com

For a complete list of our titles or to place an order
online, visit www.destinyimage.com.